TEENS & Alcohol

GAIL SNYDER

THE GALLUP YOUTH SURVEY:
MAJOR ISSUES AND TRENDS

Teens and Alcohol

Teens and Family Issues

Teens and Race

Teens, Religion, and Values

Teens and Sex

Teens and Suicide

TEENS & Alcohol

GAIL SNYDER

Produced by OTTN Publishing, Stockton, New Jersey

Mason Crest Publishers
370 Reed Road
Broomall, PA 19008
www.masoncrest.com

3 5 7 9 8 6 4 2

Library of Congress Cataloging-in-Publication Data

Snyder, Gail.
   Teens and alcohol / Gail Snyder.
     p. cm. — (The Gallup Youth Survey, major issues and trends)
Summary: Uses data from the Gallup Youth Survey and other sources to
examine issues related to teenage drinking.
Includes bibliographical references and index.
   ISBN 1-59084-723-7
1. Teenagers—Alcohol use—United States—Juvenile literature.
2. Alcoholism—United States—Juvenile literature. 3. Drinking of
alcoholic beverages—United States—Juvenile literature. [1. Teenagers—
Alcohol use. 2. Alcoholism.] I. Title. II. Series.
   HV5135.S64 2004
   362.292'2'08350973—dc22
                                    2003018380

Contents

Introduction

By George Gallup

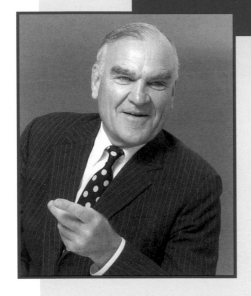

As the United States moves into the new century, there is a vital need for insight into what it means to be a young person in America. Today's teenagers—the so-called "Y Generation"—will be the leaders and shapers of the 21st century. The future direction of the United States is being determined now in their hearts and minds and actions. Yet how much do we as a society know about this important segment of the U.S. populace who have the potential to lift our nation to new levels of achievement and social health?

The nation's teen population will top 30 million by the year 2006, the highest number since 1975. Most of these teens will grow up to be responsible citizens and leaders. But some youths face very long odds against reaching adulthood physically safe, behaviorally sound, and economically self-supporting. The challenges presented to society by the less fortunate youth are enormous. To help meet these challenges it is essential to have an accurate picture of the present status of teenagers.

The Gallup Youth Survey—the oldest continuing survey of teenagers—exists to help society meet its responsibility to youth, as well as to inform and guide our leaders by probing the social and economic attitudes and behaviors of young people. With theories abounding about the views, lifestyles, and values of adolescents, the Gallup Youth Survey, through regular scientific measurements of teen themselves, serves as a sort of reality check.

We need to hear more clearly the voices of young people, and to help them better articulate their fears and their hopes. Our youth have much to share with their elders—is the older generation really listening? Is it carefully monitoring the hopes and fears of teenagers today? Failure to do so could result in severe social consequences.

Surveys reveal that the image of teens in the United States today is a negative one. Teens are frequently maligned, misunderstood, or simply ignored by their elders. Yet two decades of the Gallup Youth Survey have provided ample evidence of the very special qualities of the nation's youngsters. In fact, if our society is less racist, less sexist, less polluted, and more peace loving, we can in considerable measure thank our young people, who have been on the leading edge on these issues.

And the younger generation is not geared to greed: survey after survey has shown that teens have a keen interest in helping those people, especially in their own communities, who are less fortunate than themselves

Young people tell the Gallup Youth Survey that they are enthusiastic about helping others, and are willing to work for world peace and a healthy world. They feel positive about their schools and even more positive about their teachers. A large majority of American teenagers report that they are happy and excited about the future, feel very close to their families, are likely to marry, want to have children, are satisfied with their personal lives, and desire to reach the top of their chosen careers.

But young adults face many threats, so parents, guardians, and concerned adults must commit themselves to do everything possible to help tomorrow's parents, citizens, and leaders avoid or overcome risky behaviors so that they can move into the future with greater hope and understanding.

The Gallup Organization and the Gallup Youth Survey are enthusiastic about this partnership with Mason Crest Publishers. Through carefully and clearly written books on a variety of vital topics dealing with teens, Gallup Youth Survey statistics are presented in a way that gives new depth and meaning to the data. The focus of these books is a practical one—to provide readers with the statistics and solid information that they need to understand and to deal with each important topic.

* * *

Alcohol use has been clearly identified as a major factor in many teen-related issues: highway deaths, accidental deaths and injuries, risky sex practices, poor school performance, depression, and suicide. The statistics are frightening. Yet many young people today are drinking illegally and irresponsibly.

Teens across the nation are at risk for alcohol-related problems. Underage drinking may lead to addiction and other physiological or psychological problems later in life. Young people who head to college without hard facts about alcohol abuse at their disposal may find themselves unprepared and vulnerable in the "drink to get drunk" environment of many campuses.

Parents and those who work with teens must be armed with the facts. This book examines alcohol and alcohol abuse among teens and in society in a comprehensive and non-judgmental way. It covers many vital topics, including myths about alcohol, signs that point to dependence, parental responsibility, and organizations that can help teens (and their families) get back on track.

Chapter One

In June 2001, twin sisters Barbara (left) and Jenna Bush (right) were cited for attempting to use false ID to obtain alcohol. The president's daughters were among a rising number of American teenagers drawn to drinking.

Even the President's Daughters Do It

In June 2001, at a Tex-Mex restaurant called Chuy's in Austin, Texas, two pretty, vivacious twin sisters walked in and ordered beers. The restaurant manager thought the 19-year-old girls looked underage so he asked them for identification. One of the girls quickly produced a driver's license. Aware that he could lose his liquor license and face a lawsuit for serving minors, he took his time looking over her I.D. Then he decided to make a phone call.

Instead of getting the beers they ordered, Jenna and Barbara got an unexpected visit from the police. Barbara, a student at Yale University, had never been arrested for underage drinking before, but her sister, then a freshman at the University of Texas in Austin, had gotten into trouble two months earlier for drinking at an Austin nightclub known as Cheers Shot Bar.

Jenna Bush, daughter of President George W. Bush, pleaded no contest to the earlier charge of

Do you have occasion to use alcoholic beverages such as liquor, wine, or beer, or are you a total abstainer?

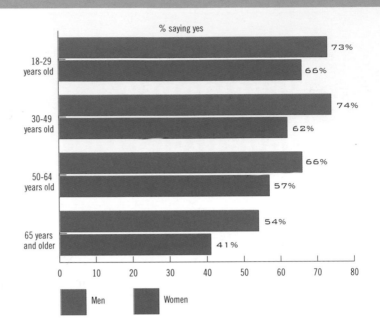

% saying yes

Age group	Men	Women
18-29 years old	73%	66%
30-49 years old	74%	62%
50-64 years old	66%	57%
65 years and older	54%	41%

Men Women

Do you sometimes drink more alcoholic beverages than you think you should?

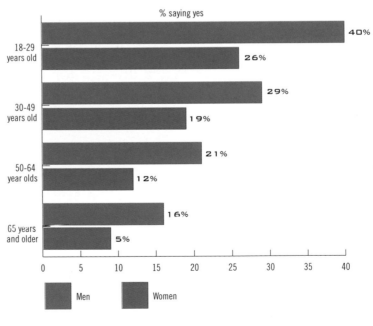

% saying yes

Age group	Men	Women
18-29 years old	40%	26%
30-49 years old	29%	19%
50-64 year olds	21%	12%
65 years and older	16%	5%

Men Women

Results based on five polls conducted between September 1999 and July 2003; 5,114 total respondents.
Source: The Gallup Organization

being a minor in possession of alcohol, and was fined $51.25. She was also ordered to serve eight hours of community service and instructed to take classes in alcohol awareness for six hours. "Good luck to you, Miss Bush," Judge Elisabeth Earle told Jenna after handing down the sentence.

Before that particular infraction, Jenna's 18-year-old boyfriend was arrested for public drunkenness in January 2001, after police raided an underage drinking party he attended. The Secret Service had to step in to bail the young man out of jail.

The public transgressions of the Bush daughters made national news and became the subject of jokes by late-night talk show hosts. Other people were more sympathetic to Jenna and Barbara. "This poor girl, I feel so sorry for her," said attorney John Wall of Jenna, whom he prosecuted for the Cheers Shot Bar incident. "She's getting all this media attention for something as commonplace as alcohol possession in a college town."

Following the violation at Chuy's, Barbara Bush was fined $100 for underage drinking while her sister, who had used a friend's driver's license in her attempt to buy the drinks, found herself hit with a $600 fine. These were minor penalties compared to what they could have been handed had it been a third offense.

Just four years before Barbara and Jenna Bush were busted for underage drinking, their father and at the time the governor of Texas signed a tough "three-strikes" state law specifically intended to crack down on young drinkers. Under the law, anybody under the age of 21 who was convicted three times of offenses related to underage drinking would automatically be sentenced to prison. "We want our young people to make healthy choices by avoiding drugs, alcohol and tobacco," Bush declared when he signed the zero tolerance law.

Bush's law could have had drastic consequences for his own daughter. Because Jenna had been caught for underage drinking on two separate occasions, she faced a term in jail if she would have been caught one more time before turning 21.

The Bush girls were trying to do what nearly 30 percent of the teens participating in a 2003 Gallup Youth Survey admitted to doing: drinking liquor, wine, or beer before their 21st birthdays. Some organizations have reported other startling statistics on underage drinking. The National Council on Alcohol and Drug Dependence estimates that 87 percent of high school seniors have used alcohol. By comparison, the council reports, only 63 percent of high school seniors have smoked cigarettes and 32 percent have tried marijuana.

Teenage Drinking on the Rise

The number of teens who admit to underage drinking has experienced a dramatic rise since 1993, according to polls conducted over the years by the Gallup Youth Survey. The Gallup Organization, a national polling firm, set up the survey as a long-term project to gauge trends among young people. In 1993, 21 percent of the teens who responded to a Gallup Youth Survey reported that on occasion, they consume either liquor, wine, or beer. By 2003, that number had risen to 29 percent—nearly a 40 percent increase.

What makes that number particularly troubling is that teenage drinking has increased even though lawmakers and civic groups have taken steps to curb the activity. In 1993, the Gallup Youth Survey reported that 48 percent of the young people who participated in a poll said that it is "very easy" for them to obtain alcoholic beverages. A decade later, just 27 percent reported that obtaining beer, wine, and liquor is "very easy."

There is no question that people are taking steps to stop under-age drinking. Legislators have stiffened the laws regulating alcohol sales to minors, police have become much more vigilant in enforcing the laws, and many parents and schools have discouraged teenage drinking. Nevertheless, even though young people reported that it was becoming much more difficult for them to obtain alcohol, the Gallup Youth Survey's results show that the number of teenagers who are drinking is still on the rise.

Joseph A. Califano Jr., former U.S. Secretary of Health, Education, and Welfare and chairman of the National Center on Addiction and Substance Abuse (CASA), sees underage drinking as a serious national issue:

> By any public health standard, America has an epidemic of underage drinking that germinates in elementary and middle schools with children 9 to 13 years old and erupts on college campuses where 44 percent of students binge drink and alcohol is the number one substance of abuse—implicated in date rape, sexual harassment, racial disturbances, dropouts, overdose deaths from alcohol poisoning and suicides. Preliminary studies have shown that alcohol damages young minds, limiting mental and social development. High schoolers who drink are five times likelier to drop out of school. No other substance threatens as many of the nation's children.

Experts have cited several dangers related to teenage drinking. The younger people are when they start drinking, they have found, the greater their chances of becoming dependent on alcohol. According to the National Clearinghouse for Alcohol and Drug Information, people who begin drinking before they are 15 years old are four times more likely to become alcoholics than people who begin drinking when they turn 21. Also, because alcohol has a more profound physical effect on young people than it does on older people, teens are more likely than adults to engage in risky sexual behavior, die in alcohol-related traffic accidents, and die from alcohol poisoning.

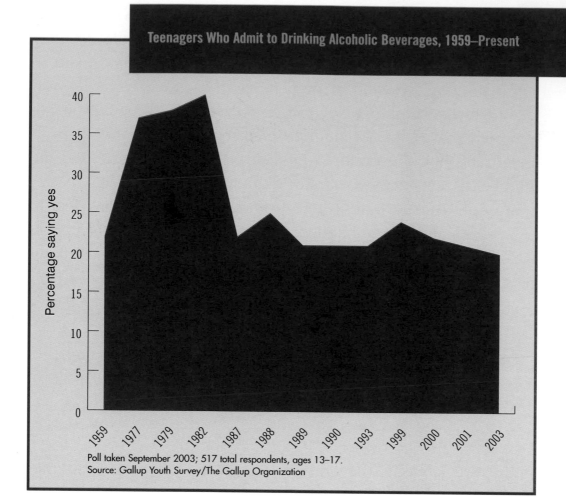

Teenagers Who Admit to Drinking Alcoholic Beverages, 1959–Present

Poll taken September 2003; 517 total respondents, ages 13–17.
Source: Gallup Youth Survey/The Gallup Organization

Many young people simply don't realize the physical dangers they face when they drink excessively. For example, alcohol eliminates the gag reflex that prevents people from choking on their own vomit—in other words, it stops the body from reacting naturally to expel a poison. Alcohol poisoning and other alcohol-related injuries claim the lives of more than 1,400 college students each year, according to an April 2002 study by the National Institutes of Health. In addition, an average of eight teenagers die in alcohol-related automobile crashes every day, according to a report by the

Center for Substance Abuse Prevention.

Early drinkers, whom some research groups define as those who begin drinking as early as age 13, place themselves at an increased risk for problems that last well into adulthood. A study by the Rand Corporation, a research group, followed 3,400 students in California and Oregon for a decade. The students were interviewed in 7th grade, 12th grade, and at age 23. During the final series of interviews, many students who had been early drinkers admitted to missing work, being dependent on cigarettes, alcohol, or drugs, and having criminal records.

According to the National Council on Alcohol and Drug Dependence, 7 percent of 8th graders, 18 percent of 10th graders, and 30 percent of 12th graders say they not only drink at least once a month, but that they also drink to the point of intoxication. The council reported that teens who binge drink

Hollywood actress Drew Barrymore, who became a star as a young girl, is a recovering alcoholic. She began drinking at age 10.

say they do so because they are lonely, upset, bored, or looking for ways to have fun.

Hollywood actress Drew Barrymore, whose movie credits include *E.T.*, *Riding in Cars with Boys*, and *Charlie's Angels*, is a former alcoholic. She described how her drinking problem began when she was just 10 years old: "I started drinking with friends when I slept over at their houses. Just sneaking a drink here, a beer there. After a while, though, drinking became the only way I thought I could have fun. Only I didn't drink to have fun. I drank to get drunk."

How do underage drinkers obtain beer, wine, and spirits in the first place? There are three common ways: they obtain it with false identification, as the Bush twins attempted to do; they talk an adult into supplying them with alcohol; or they raid their parents' liquor cabinet at home or even slip into a neighbor's garage, where a case of beer may be stored.

A young girl named Miranda, whose last name is being withheld because she is a minor, remembered her early drinking experiences:

> The first time I drank I was at my friend Mike's house. I was over there one Friday night, and we figured we'd give it a try. His dad had some beer around, so we drank that; I had one and a half beers. I don't know; it just seemed like a cool thing to try. . . . Anyway, I drank a couple times more after that, on and off. And by the time I was in seventh grade, I was drinking a lot. It was every weekend for sure and once or twice during the school week. . . . No one in my family was a drinker, so I couldn't get any from home.

Miranda's story, Drew Barrymore's bout with alcohol addiction, and the legal troubles that the Bush sisters faced illustrate the universal appeal of underage drinking as well as its dangers. Young people in inner-city neighborhoods drink before reaching the age of 21, as do middle-class kids who attend suburban high schools, and young movie stars and the children of national leaders. Underage drinkers may face a number of potential problems, including the dangers of binge drinking on college campuses, drinking and driving, and other types of risky behavior. Other hotly debated issues on this topic concern prevention and treatment, such as how ads on TV and other media outlets promote teenage drinking, and what type of treatments are available to teen alcoholics.

Chapter Two

Underage drinkers often fail to effectively monitor their own drinking. Many teens are not aware that liquor and wine have higher levels of alcohol than beer, a point of confusion that can have drastic results.

Alcohol and Its Dangers Through the Ages

Perhaps the most common thread among teenagers who drink is a lack of information about how to drink responsibly and in moderation. In a Gallup Youth Survey released in 1999, 9 percent of teens between the ages of 13 and 17 reported that they "drink more alcohol than they should." A similar Gallup Youth Survey taken that year asked teen drinkers, "Do you, yourself, every worry that you may have a problem with alcohol?" An astounding 96 percent of teens who drink admitted that they fear becoming problem drinkers.

Monitoring one's own drinking is a problem shared by people of all age groups. A central difficulty lies in the fact that beverages have different levels of alcohol. Whiskey is typically 40 percent alcohol by volume, as are most rums, gins, and vodkas. Beer, on the other hand, is only on average 4.5 percent alcohol by volume and wine 11 percent. By way of comparison, a one-and-a-half ounce glass of whiskey contains the same amount of alcohol found in 12 ounces of beer and 5 ounces of wine.

A combination of hydrogen, oxygen, and carbon may sound fairly harmless, but those are the chemical building blocks that make up ethanol, or ethyl alcohol—the type of alcohol found in beer, wine, and liquor. In its purest form alcohol is odorless and colorless. To make alcohol all one has to do is combine microscopic fungi called yeasts with sugar to kick off a process known as fermentation.

Wine is made from fermented grapes while beer is made from cereal grain that has been brewed before it is fermented. Liquor undergoes the additional process of distillation, in which the fermented juice or grain is heated until it produces a vapor that yields pure alcohol when cooled. Pure alcohol is extremely dangerous to drink. Most alcoholic beverages contain no more than 40 percent alcohol.

In the United States, the alcohol content of wine and liquor is measured by a system known as "proof spirit," which is displayed on the label of the bottle. The reported proof strength is twice as high as the alcohol content. In another words, an 80 proof bottle of scotch is 40 percent alcohol. Outside the United States, alcohol content is measured differently—in Great Britain and France, for example, the alcohol content of liquor and wine is stated by volume. Thus a bottle that is labeled 45 percent alcohol content is, as the label reports, 45 percent alcohol.

What Alcohol Does to the Body

People who do not know exactly what they are drinking may be placing themselves in extreme danger. Drinking does more than induce a temporary warm and happy feeling. It also affects the stomach, liver, kidneys, and brain in adverse ways. When alcohol enters the digestive system, the stomach takes the initial hit. If the person didn't eat first, the alcohol is likely to irritate the stomach's lining and may cause the drinker to vomit. The presence of food helps the body absorb the spirits better. The stomach absorbs about 20 percent of the alcohol, and the small intestine absorbs the rest. At that point, the chemical is carried to every tissue in the body by the bloodstream except fatty tissue, which cannot break down alcohol. Because men have less fat in their bodies than women, they tend to hold their liquor better than women even if a male drinker and female drinker weigh the same and are identical in height.

One of the worst physical effects of drinking too much alcohol is the hangover, whose symptoms include dehydration, nausea, and headaches. Teenage drinkers may experience more intense hangovers than adult drinkers.

People who drink alcohol usually find they have to make many trips to the bathroom. That's because alcohol decreases the kidney's ability to absorb water. About 10 percent of the alcohol is removed through urination and breathing. The liver processes the rest of the alcohol, breaking it down into acetic acid, water, and carbon dioxide. It takes the average person one hour to rid his body of a 12-ounce can of beer, but if more beer than that has been consumed during that time, the body will fall behind. That's how people get drunk.

One unpleasant side effect of drinking is the hangover, which usually shows up the day after an episode of heavy drinking. Characterized usually by a pounding headache, a fuzzy tongue, and a sick feeling in the stomach, a hangover is the body's way of discouraging excessive drinking.

Alcohol drains the body of water that needs to be replaced before the hangover sufferer can feel better. Along with causing dehydration, it leaves behind impurities known as *cogeners*, which cause headaches, nausea, and the other symptoms of the hangover. Fewer impurities are found in colorless drinks like gin, vodka, and white wine; as one might expect, the hangovers from drinking these beverages are not quite as bad as what people can expect to experience from drinking red wine, port, and sherry. There is only one way to recover from a hangover and that is to give the body time to return to its equilibrium. Kidneys and lungs take about 18 to 24 hours to restore the body's blood acid levels to their normal levels after a bout of drinking.

While a hangover is a nuisance, the damages that can occur to the drinker's brain during a binge can be deadly. The part of the brain that is first affected by alcohol is the cerebral cortex, located in the front of the brain. It processes information and makes voluntary body movements possible. When a certain amount of alcohol reaches the cerebral cortex, the drinker loses his or her inhibitions and has difficulty thinking, seeing, hearing, smelling, and experiencing pain.

When alcohol reaches the part of the brain known as the limbic system, memory and emotion are affected. Drinkers with distressed limbic systems are more easily angered, upset, and withdrawn. Next they lose their fine motor coordination, regulated by the part of the brain known as the cerebellum. When drivers are pulled over under suspicion of being drunk, the police officer conducts what is known as a field sobriety test to check for impaired motor coordination, asking suspects to close their eyes and touch their fingers to their nose.

Finally, if a drinker consumes a tremendous amount of alcohol, the part of the brain that controls breathing, consciousness, heart rate, and temperature—the medulla—can be compromised. This may result in a decreased breathing rate, a drop in body temperature and blood pressure, a loss of consciousness and, finally, death.

Scientists have conducted research on the effects of alcohol on the brains of young drinkers. Dr. Sandra Brown, chief of psychology services at the Veterans Affairs Medical Center in San Diego, headed a research study for the American Medical Association that compared the brains of 14- to 21-year-old alcohol abusers with those of young people who do not drink. Using magnetic resonance imaging, Brown and her team discovered that the brains of drinkers had significantly shrunk in the area that controls memory and learning. She also found that adults would have to consume twice as much liquor as teenagers do to receive the same amount of damage to their brains.

"Our brains go through important transformations during adolescence," Brown said. "This study shows that alcohol use during the adolescent years is associated with damage to memory and learning capabilities as well as to the decision-making and reasoning areas in the brain."

In addition to the brain, other major organs can suffer damage from excessive drinking. One of the most common ailments attributed to heavy drinking is cirrhosis, a complication that affects the liver. The liver of a cirrhosis sufferer becomes scarred by the organ's constant exposure to alcohol. Among the symptoms that result from cirrhosis are internal bleeding and swollen ankles, caused by the liver's inability to expel salt. Cirrhosis can even result in brain damage, which manifests itself in loss of memory, disorientation, or even coma. The condition can be fatal.

Alcohol Through the Centuries

Hangovers, alcohol poisoning, cirrhosis of the liver, and other ill effects of drinking are maladies that have afflicted heavy drinkers for as long as people have consumed alcoholic beverages. For centuries, society has known about the consequences of drinking and has made attempts to warn individuals about the dangers. In 1629, for example, the Virginia Colonial Assembly established one of the first liquor-control laws in America when it admonished ministers to set a good example for churchgoers by refraining from excessive alcohol use.

Archaeologists have found evidence of the drinking of alcoholic beverages among ancient artifacts. Stone tablets carved in the year 4000 B.C. by a Middle Eastern people known as the Sumerians show images of bread being baked, crumbled into water to form mash, made into a drink and, finally, consumed. Archaeologists also found a written message, dated around 2000 B.C., in which an Egyptian father offers his son advice on how to live his life and a warning about the dangers of drinking beer. Much of his message has survived the centuries. Its translation reads: "Love writing, hate dancing, and do not set your heart on playing. Keep away from beer and girls."

If it were possible to sample beer or wine from ancient times, it would probably not taste at all like their modern-day versions. Ancient beer, for example, had to be consumed within days of its production or it would turn to vinegar. In addition, it is likely that the alcohol would have been made from unconventional sources. The Chinese made wine from rice. Africans made wine from bananas, honey, corn, millet, and other fruits. Native Americans made wine from cactus plants. In Mexico, the Aztecs produced a drink they called *pulque* by fermenting juice from the maguey cactus. *Pulque* packed a kick, but tasted like sour milk.

Sometimes people drank beer and wine for health reasons. If the local water supply was poor, alcohol was one form of substitute. Sailors, who were susceptible to scurvy, found protection from the disease by the vitamin C content of beer. The sailors' passage through ports near and far helped to spread beer around the world.

Around A.D. 776, an Arabian alchemist named Jabir ibn Haiyan invented the process of distillation to create the first liquor. Around the year 1300, the Spanish physician and alchemist Arnoldus Villanovanus created the first brandy as a health elixir. The German author Hieronymus Braunschweig wrote a book in 1519 with instructions on the art of distillation. As the process of distilling liquor became widespread, people used whatever materials were handy to create gin, vodka, whiskey, rye, tequila, and rum. People implemented fermented barley and potatoes, rye and

Two African American boys stand in the sugarcane field of a Louisiana plantation. African slave labor was once exploited for the harvesting of sugar, much of which was used to manufacture rum.

corn, sugar cane and molasses, and cacti in ways previously unimagined.

A slave trade even developed from the heavy demand for rum. Workers were needed to harvest sugarcane on plantations located in the West Indies. Africans sold into slavery were transported on English ships to the plantations; those same ships then carried the molasses produced from slave labor to New England, where it was distilled into rum. Barrels of rum were then loaded on ships bound for Africa, where it would be sold and the profits could be used to buy more slaves.

Native Americans were making beer before the Pilgrims arrived on the Mayflower in 1620. Early Americans regarded drinking alcohol as a healthy pastime, and those who suffered from indigestion, pain, and other health complaints made themselves feel better with alcohol. Colonial laws encouraged the brewing and consumption of beer because of its modest alcohol content. Travelers in colonial America could always count on finding a tavern at a crossroads. Martin Van Buren, eighth president of the United States, grew up the son of an innkeeper in Kinderhook, New York, and spent much of his youth serving beer and ale to thirsty travelers.

Prohibition and Its Repeal

In the early 20th century, public opinion about alcohol changed as groups like the Anti-Saloon

Martin Van Buren, the eighth U.S. president, spent his adolescence as a bartender at his father's inn. During the early decades of U.S. history, travelers frequented drinking establishments like taverns and inns.

A man kneels by a sign pointing the way to a speakeasy, a kind of underground nightclub that served alcohol during the Prohibition years. Alcohol was prohibited in the United States between 1920 and 1933, though many people found ways to drink illegally.

League and the Women's Temperance Movement began flexing their political muscles. Dissatisfied with the rapid expansion of American saloons, in which drinking was often accompanied by gambling and prostitution, temperance groups were instrumental in passing the 18th Amendment to the Constitution. This amendment—as well as its enforcement arm, known as the Volstead Act—banned the production, sale, and consumption of alcohol in the United States.

Prohibition proved to be failure, and early signs of its demise appeared even before the 18th Amendment went into effect on January 16, 1920. Three months earlier, a half-million gallons of alcohol were stolen out of government warehouses. In Chicago, within six months of the start of Prohibition, the courts were swollen with Volstead Act violations. The era, known as the Roaring Twenties, saw the rise of organized crime in the United States. Gangsters such as Al Capone and Lucky Luciano became big-time bootleggers, illegally importing or manufacturing their own booze. Underground nightclubs called speakeasies opened by the thousands in most major cities.

In 1929, the stock market crashed, soon plunging the United States into the Great Depression. Overnight, hundreds of thousands of Americans were out of work. Many people became homeless, living in tent cities known as Hoovervilles, named mockingly after President Herbert Hoover, who seemed incapable of rescuing the country from economic hardship. In the cities, people would line up for several blocks to receive free handouts of bread and soup.

By early 1932, it didn't seem terribly important anymore to continue enforcing an unpopular temperance law at a time when so many people were more concerned with how to feed their families. In 1930 the U.S. Justice Department conservatively estimated that Americans were consuming some 73 million gallons of alcoholic beverages a year. At the 1932 Democratic National Convention in Chicago, presidential nominee Franklin D. Roosevelt pledged to repeal Prohibition. He said, "This convention wants repeal. Your candidate wants repeal. And I am confident that the United States of America wants repeal."

Certainly, Roosevelt had his eye on more than just winning votes when he opposed the unpopular law. He knew that the government could raise vast sums of money by taxing alcohol—money that would help fund the New Deal social programs he was planning to implement. Roosevelt went on that year to defeat President Hoover. Within weeks of his inauguration in 1933, the repeal amendment was passed in the House and the Senate. State legislatures, which must approve amendments to the Constitution, quickly acted as well, and on December 5, 1933, the 21st Amendment to the Constitution became law.

The Legal Drinking Age

Following the repeal of Prohibition, most states established 21 as the Minimum Legal Drinking Age, or MLDA. During the 1960s, though, Congress enacted a draft of men as young as 18 to supply troops to the Vietnam War. When the young men returned from duty overseas, they had two complaints: first, they should be old enough to vote, and second, they should be old enough to legally buy a drink. Many people believed these complaints were valid, especially since the government considered the young men old enough to die for their country.

Congress responded by lowering the voting age to 18. Many of the states, which regulate alcohol sales, responded by lowering the legal drinking age. The effects of the lower drinking age soon became evident, particularly on the highways. Drunken driving by young people became a major national concern. Studies found that most young people do not drink responsibly, and in 1976, states began to raise their MLDAs.

In 1984, Congress passed the Uniform Drinking Age Act, which mandated that the federal government withhold highway funds from any state that did not raise its MLDA to 21. Because states rely heavily on the federal government to supply money for road construction and repair, the remaining states with an MLDA below 21 raised their minimum drinking ages, although some states delayed implementing the law for many years. In Louisiana, where the economy of New Orleans depends largely on the party atmosphere of the French Quarter, officials managed to wait until 1995 to raise the MLDA.

Since the minimum legal drinking age was raised, there has been a drop in the number of alcohol-related automobile deaths. The National Traffic Safety Administration reported a 43 percent drop in these fatalities for people under 21 during the years

American drivers under the age of 21 will receive a fine or other punishment if they are found to have consumed any alcohol. During the 1960s and the 1970s, the Minimum Legal Drinking Age (MLDA) in many states was 18, though all the states have since raised it to 21.

between 1987 and 1996. During the same period, there was a 28 percent decline in alcohol-related traffic fatalities among the general population.

Not surprisingly, over the years adults have generally supported keeping the drinking age at 21 while teens have favored lowering the drinking age. In 1979, as state legislators first started raising the MLDAs, the Gallup Youth Survey reported that as many as 70 percent of young people in states with low MLDAs preferred keeping the age where it was—at 18 or 19. And in states with an MLDA of 21, 37 percent of the respondents called for the legal drinking age to be lowered. In 2001, the Gallup Organization polled adults on the question of enacting harsher penalties for underage drinkers. The survey found that 60 percent of the respondents believe the penalties for underage drinking should be stricter, while 77 percent said they opposed lowering the legal drinking age to 18.

Buying and possessing alcohol is a crime in every state in the United States for people who are under 21. Yet young people consume 3.6 billion drinks a year, the equivalent of 10 million a day. Middle school and high school students drink 1.1 billion cans of beer a year and 35 percent of all wine coolers sold in the United States. Wine coolers have the same alcohol content as wine but taste like soda, with high concentrations of fruit juice and sugar.

Because the United States has the highest legal drinking age in the Western world, the legal drinking age remains a controversial topic. Teenagers in such countries as Austria, Great Britain, and Switzerland can begin drinking alcohol in public at 16. In many of Canada's provinces, young adults only need to be 18 or 19 to drink legally. People who believe that the drinking age should be lowered in the United States argue that it is frequently ignored by teens anyway, and that parents should be given the task of teaching young people how to handle alcohol in a responsible manner.

Ruth C. Engs, professor of applied health at Indiana University, is among those pushing to lower the minimum legal drinking age to 18 or 19. She believes teenagers find drinking even more attractive because it is illegal, and that if it were legal for teens to drink at home and in restaurants with their parents looking on, they would be less likely to abuse alcohol. The professor argues that many ethnic groups, including Greeks, Italians, Chinese, and Jews, regard drinking wine as a traditional family rite, and that many children raised in such environments go on to have few drinking problems as adults.

"Alcohol is neither seen as a poison or a magic potion," said Dr. Engs. "There is little or no social pressure to drink, irresponsible behavior is never tolerated, young people learn at home from their parents and other adults how to handle alcohol in a responsible manner, there is societal consensus on what constitutes responsible drinking." However, the American Medical Association points out that the lower drinking age in Europe has not made for a healthier population. According to studies, Europeans have similar or higher rates of cirrhosis of the liver than Americans.

Chapter Three

As teenagers get older, particularly when they attend college, peer pressure factors more in their decision to drink alcohol.

Giving in to the Pressure

Scott Krueger was an excellent student with good grades and top college board scores. He won admission to the freshman class at Massachusetts Institute of Technology, and at the beginning of his first semester in 1997, began pledging to a fraternity. One particular initiation meeting that Krueger attended involved hard drinking. Unaware of the grave dangers of excessive drinking, he consumed 16 straight shots of whiskey.

When his friends discovered him passed out on the floor, it was already too late. At the hospital he was put on life support until his parents and physicians concluded that he had no hope of recovery. "We sent our son to MIT for five weeks," said Scott's mother, Darlene, "and . . . picked him up in a box and took him back in the back of my station wagon."

Many teenagers feel pressured to drink because their friends drink. Any high school student at a beer party knows what peer pressure is like when friends begin splitting up a six-pack. Over the years, many mental health organizations have studied peer pressure and found that it is one of the main causes of underage drinking. In 2003, the National Institute on Alcohol Abuse and Alcoholism issued a report concluding that based on their findings, "the most reliable predictor of a youth's drinking behavior is the drinking behavior of his or her friends. Positive beliefs about alcohol's effects and the social acceptability of drinking encourage the adolescent to begin and continue drinking."

The Gallup Youth Survey has also examined how peer pressure affects young people and has discovered that as teens grow older, they are more likely to give in to peer pressure. In 1978, a Gallup report found that alcohol was served at 34 percent of parties attended by teenagers between the ages of 16 and 18. Also, 27 percent of the teens who hosted parties said their friends would be less likely to attend if alcoholic beverages were not served. In contrast, drinking took place at just 10 percent of the parties attended by teenage respondents aged 15 and younger.

In a 2003 Gallup Youth Survey, 42 percent of teenagers aged 16 and 17 reported using alcohol. The survey also showed that 22 percent of teens between the ages of 13 and 15 had experimented with alcohol. Rick Blizzard, a health care consultant to the Gallup Organization, believed that peer pressure could well have been the primary cause of the significant increase between the two age groups.

Alcohol in the Media

Friends aren't the only ones who influence a teenager's decision to drink alcohol. Parents have an impact on teenagers' choices, and in many situations they do not set a great example or give valuable advice. The media can be another potentially negative influence, as each day teenagers are inundated with images and sounds that encourage alcohol use. Most television viewers would agree that beer advertisements are aimed at a young audience. The Canadian beer company Labatt Blue has employed a hockey-playing bear as a spokesman for its products. The Anheuser-Busch brand Bud Ice has relied on singing penguins to get the attention of commercial viewers.

Those commercials and others featuring young singles partying on the beach suggest that marketers aim beer advertisements

Comic movie star Will Ferrell drinks from a beer funnel after delivering a speech at Harvard University. Researchers have drawn correlations between underage drinking and the pro-drinking examples set in films, television shows, and commercials.

at an age group that includes teenagers. Researchers at a Berkeley, California–based alcohol and drug research institute would back up this claim. In 1998, the Prevention Research Center conducted a study on the effect of alcohol advertising on young people. "What we found is the more kids like the ads, and as a result, they pay attention to them, the more likely they are to be drinkers and the more often they drink," said researcher Joel Grube.

The Prevention Research Center studied how 470 San Francisco–area students in grades 7 through 10 responded to beer advertising on television. "The two attributes that seemed to be getting kids' attention were humor and ads that had youth-oriented music—rock, country-western or, in one case, hip-hop," said Grube.

Many Americans are consumers at heart and want the latest clothing, technology, and music. If they can't afford to buy it, they dream about what life would be like if they could. Television shows and commercials, newspapers and magazines, music videos, and Internet sites deliver an unending array of messages about what is cool and trendy. Advertisers know the average teenager has about $50 a week to spend. With their allowance in hand or money they earned at their first jobs, teens are eager consumers and are receptive to advertising. Even though they are too young to drink legally, they are regularly exposed to alcohol advertising and its implicit message that drinking brings popularity and success. Many teens are paying close attention.

Judging by the many hours that research shows teens spend watching TV, there is no question that they are at least susceptible to alcohol advertising. In 2003, a Gallup Youth Survey gauged the average number of hours teens spend in front of the TV every week. The survey reported that 67 percent of youths between the ages of 13 and 15 spend between 5 and 20 or more hours a week watching TV; 54 percent of those aged 16 and 17 spend the same amount of time in front of the television. The American Psychological Association estimated that by the time children have graduated from high school, they have seen 22,000 hours of TV—about twice as much time spent in the classroom.

During this time in front of the TV, many teenagers are watching commercials. In 2002, the marketing-research firm Teenage Research Unlimited asked teenagers to pick their favorite TV ads. Named most often were Budweiser commercials, which drew more attention than commercials for Pepsi, Nike, and Levi's jeans. Beer is the most commonly advertised beverage on television, and in 2001, brewers spent $695 million to air their commercials.

Researchers say that teenagers watch about 20,000 commercials a year, and 10 percent of those are touting alcoholic drinks. There are few TV commercials for hard liquor, however. For decades, distillers of whiskey, gin, and other spirits have voluntarily agreed to keep their ads off TV. Commercials for spirits do surface from time to time, though in general only on cable TV. Researchers estimate that overall, distillers spend less than $1 million a year on TV advertising. Even without the distillers, however, alcohol commercials outnumber anti-drinking public service ads by 50 to 1. More television commercials featuring alcohol are viewed by 12- to 20-year-olds than commercials advertising juices, sodas, snack foods, sneakers, and jeans.

In 1999 researchers at the University of Michigan interviewed children and adults about alcohol advertising. The researchers found that a majority of middle school and high school students felt that beer and alcohol advertisers were trying to reach them with their commercials. Adults also expressed the opinion that alcohol advertising could influence teenagers. Three-quarters of

To avoid the risk of attracting teenage drinkers, hard alcohol companies like Maker's Mark have agreed to restrict the airing of television commercials, instead focusing on roadside billboards and other advertising outlets.

adults polled by the University of Michigan stated that the ads make drinking seem desirable to teens.

Among the favorite networks of young adults are Comedy Central, BET, and ESPN, all of which have been cited by the Center on Alcohol Marketing and Youth at Georgetown University in Washington for exposing young viewers to excessive alcohol advertising. On ESPN, over $22 million in alcohol advertising was spent in 2001.

Advertising Guidelines

The Center on Alcohol Marketing and Youth maintains that the voluntary guidelines used by alcohol manufacturers are not strong enough to protect young people from exposure to inappropriate advertising. Current guidelines adopted by the industry ask their members to restrict ads from appearing on television shows in which at least half the audience is made up of children. Children normally make up 15 percent of the national broadcast audience. Only about 1 percent of more than 14,000 network and cable television programs have high enough concentrations of children viewers for the guidelines to apply to them.

Televised sports do not have such guidelines, yet telecasts have a high concentration of young viewers. It is hard to imagine watching a football game and not seeing advertisements for beer. For years, beer companies have maintained lucrative relationships with professional sports leagues and the networks that televise them. Beer companies find most of their consumers through televised sports. Anheuser-Busch, for example, lends its name and financial support to everything from women's basketball and triathlon competitions to hockey and auto racing.

Familiar as the link between sports and alcohol has become, it is nevertheless an oddball marriage. Far from enhancing athletic performance, alcohol actually diminishes it. Erwin Kaussner, author of *High Performance for Champions — A New Vision of Sports Nutrition*, explains why beer advertising and professional sports are an unhealthy pairing:

> [O]ffering alcohol in conjunction with a sports event or activity is more than just a mistake. As a popular national product, beer might provide a few congenial hours and a pleasant taste for non-athletes. But as a sports drink is not simply unsuitable—it is absolutely counterproductive. . . . Often I have seen young athletes—in their teenage years—who come running toward me after a match with a beer in their hand. It's written all over their face: "We're really cool, we're drinking beer now."

Kaussner also says beer diminishes minerals, trace elements, vitamins, and enzymes that are crucial to an athlete's body. It

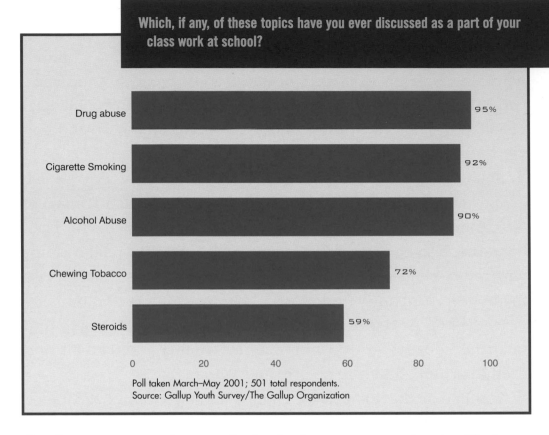

Which, if any, of these topics have you ever discussed as a part of your class work at school?

Topic	Percentage
Drug abuse	95%
Cigarette Smoking	92%
Alcohol Abuse	90%
Chewing Tobacco	72%
Steroids	59%

Poll taken March–May 2001; 501 total respondents.
Source: Gallup Youth Survey/The Gallup Organization

deadens nerves and stops the body from regenerating itself after a vigorous workout. It also causes injuries and can slow down the healing process.

Not everyone agrees that advertising encourages teens to drink who would not otherwise. David Hanson, a sociology professor and author of *Teen Alcoholism*, argues that teenagers are more likely to see alcohol portrayed on television programs than on commercials. According to a study of prime time TV, alcohol appears five times more in programming than in commercials. "Perhaps those who want to reduce the presence of alcohol on television should propose eliminating the programming and let children watch commercials instead," Hanson said. Despite the heavy presence of alcohol advertising on TV, he wonders if decreasing alcohol advertising—or removing it altogether—would really be a practical way to address the problem. "If we treat beverage alcohol as a dangerous substance to be avoided and not even advertised," he says, "we inadvertently raise it up from the ordinary into the realm of the powerful, the tantalizing, and the desirable Big Deal."

Before

After

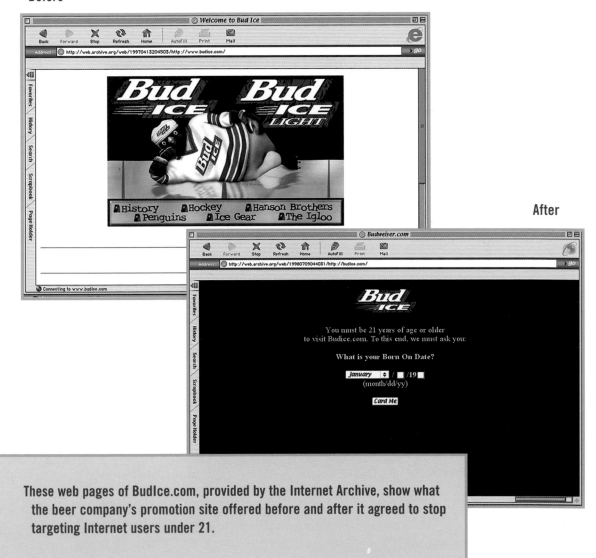

These web pages of BudIce.com, provided by the Internet Archive, show what the beer company's promotion site offered before and after it agreed to stop targeting Internet users under 21.

Laurie Leiber, former director of the Center on Alcohol Advertising, argues that more regulation should be placed on advertising aimed at underage drinkers. She believes that the public cannot trust the manufacturers to make the right marketing decisions. "The manufacturers are well aware that maintaining industry profits depends on 'recruiting' young drinkers," Leiber said. She and other researchers have found that beer companies compete for a dominant sector of the market described as "heavy drinkers," which are mostly composed of young people. According to Leiber, this situation has had adverse ramifications on marketing plans. "Because nearly half of all young people in the U.S. begin drinking before they have graduated from junior high," she said, "competition for market share among the next group of heavy drinkers means attracting people well below the drinking age."

The message that "alcohol is cool" shows up in the most unexpected places. Even a trip to the convenience store, supermarket, or gas station can expose teenagers to point-of-purchase advertisements for alcoholic beverages. In a study of more than 300 communities by the U.S. Centers for Disease Control and Prevention, signs promoting specific alcoholic beverages were found in 94 percent of the 3,961 retailers. Many of these messages are placed at child-level height. The CDC has expressed fears that aggressive alcohol advertising in stores frequented by teenagers could increase drinking and driving.

Teenagers don't even have to leave home to discover the appeal of alcohol. A 1998 Stanford University study found a relationship between teenage drinking and watching music videos or playing video games. The study, published in the journal *Pediatrics*, followed 1,533 ninth-grade students in San Jose, California, for 18 months. The teenagers were asked to record how many hours that they were exposed to some form of media (watching TV/music videos, playing computer/video games) and how many drinks they had consumed.

Researchers discovered that teens who watched just one extra

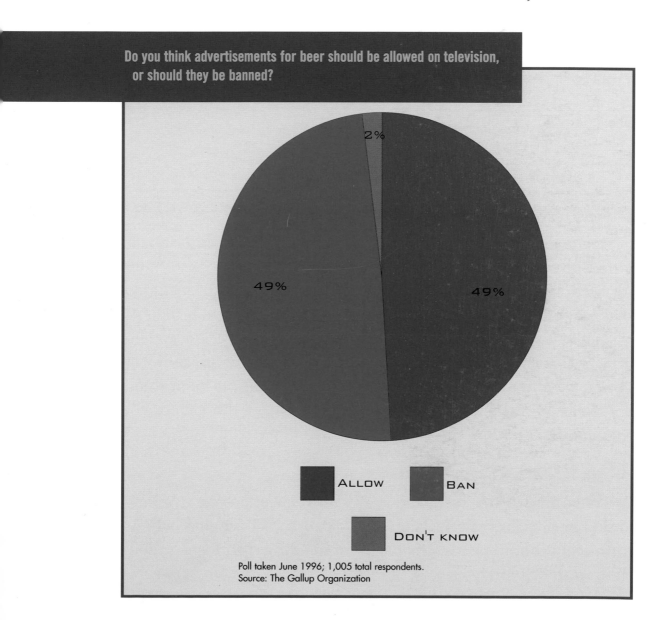

Do you think advertisements for beer should be allowed on television, or should they be banned?

2%

49%

49%

ALLOW BAN

DON'T KNOW

Poll taken June 1996; 1,005 total respondents.
Source: The Gallup Organization

hour of television reported a 9 percent average increased risk of starting to drink alcohol over the next 18 months. For each additional hour of music videos watched per day, teens had a 31 percent average increased risk of starting to drink.

Sometimes the pro-drinking message in popular music is only implicated; sometimes it's anything but subtle. Consider, for example, the lyrics to the song "Got Me a Bottle" by rap superstar 50 Cent:

> Hennessy sippin' (got me a bottle)
> Bacardi drinking (got me a bottle)
> Smirnoff sippin' (got me a bottle)
> Absolut shorty (got me a bottle)
> Tanqueray sippin' (got me a bottle)
> Absolut drinking' (got me a bottle)
> E&J sippin' (got me a bottle)
> Champagne drinkin' (got me a bottle)
> I'm gettin' tipsy off a bottle of Bacardi
> Wit' a model at a party

Teenagers who prefer surfing the Internet to watching music videos may still encounter alcohol advertising. In 1998, the Center for Media Education looked at 77 alcohol web sites and concluded that 62 percent appeared to be purposely drawing young people to them by using cartoon figures, games, and teen-friendly language. "It seems to me that it's an overall strategy of appealing to young people not old enough to drink, and enticing them to do so," said Kathryn C. Montgomery, president of the Center for Media Education.

The Parents' Role

As strong as the correlations are between underage drinking and peer pressure or television, many people believe that parents ultimately should be responsible for dissuading their teenage children from drinking.

In his book *Teen Alcoholism*, David Hanson puts forward this argument regarding parents. He cites a poll in which youths between the ages of 12 and 17 ranked the importance of six factors that could influence whether or not they drank. Peer pressure—or what their friends thought—was selected by only 28 percent of those surveyed, and only 4 percent chose advertising. By far, the most important influence on their lives was parents, chosen by 62 percent of the respondents.

Other reports confirm these conclusions about parenting and teenage drinking. A Gallup Youth Survey in August 2000 found that 93 percent of 13- to 17-year-olds agreed that their families had either a great deal of influence or some influence on them. A White House Conference on Teenagers held in May 2000 found that 15- and 16-year-olds who don't eat dinner with their parents most nights are twice as likely to drink as teenagers who enjoy regular family dinners.

Dr. Lynn Ponton, a psychiatrist and professor at the University of California at San Francisco, explains what can happen when families do not spend time together:

> Across the United States boys and girls come home after school to empty houses. No surprise, they are lonely and don't want to be alone. Friends join them, but even together they are often bored. They watch endless television and music videos or cruise the Internet looking for excitement. Smoking, drug use, and drinking can easily become a part of this picture.

There are some parents who resign themselves to the fact that their children will drink. Parents may allow underage drinking to take place in their homes. They feel that their children are safer drinking at home, or they simply may be seeking their children's admiration. But whether it is a celebration to mark prom night or a high school graduation, supplying alcohol to underage drinkers is against the law, and parents who do so risk being arrested.

Some parents who have hosted these kinds of parties have

experienced disasters. The police force of Bethlehem, Pennsylvania, discovered that 45-year-old mother Constance Weber hosted a drinking party in her home for her 16-year-old son and his friends. At the party, a 15-year-old drank himself into a coma with a blood alcohol concentration that was four times the legal driving limit. Weber, who is a nurse, spent a half-hour trying to revive the boy before she called paramedics. She faced charges of corruption of minors, endangering the welfare of children, reckless endangerment, and furnishing alcohol to minors.

Another mother faced equally severe consequences for her failed judgment. In September 2003, Megan Smith pleaded guilty to three counts of corruption of minors and one count each of endangering the welfare of children and the intimidation of a witness. Police charged her with hosting an alcohol party for 25 ninth-graders, at which Smith's 18-year-old son allegedly raped a drunk 14-year-old girl.

The lenient attitudes of some parents toward drinking may take a while to change, but widespread publicity of cases like those of Weber and Smith are bound to have an impact. Gary Tennis, legislative liaison for the Pennsylvania District Attorneys Association, said, "Increasingly, people are becoming aware that they can be subject to a criminal prosecution or a whopping lawsuit for underage drinking on the part of their children and their children's friends. Now, it's becoming less tolerable than it used to be."

In March 2003, the Kansas state senate passed one of the toughest social-host laws in the country. Under the bill, parents face six months' jail time for allowing underage children to drink at their homes—even if the parents do not supply the alcohol. Massachusetts, Minnesota, and Texas have similar laws.

A 17-year-old boy's drunken driving death was the impetus for the Kansas bill. Riggs had been drinking at a party supervised by adults prior to his accident. Debbie Riggs, the boy's mother, was shocked to learn that if a party took place in a parents' home, they would not necessarily be charged with a crime. "Parents can get out of it by saying they didn't know," she said. "With the current law, you have to prove that the parents actually handed them the beer or the drink. It makes me so mad, because they would have to be deaf, dumb and blind not to know that 40 kids were drinking on their property."

In some cases, communities are starting to enforce laws that had been ignored before. Groups like the American Medical

Teenage drinking often begins at home, in the hours after school and before parents come home from work. Many young people decide to try drinking simply because they are bored.

Association's coalition to reduce underage drinking now have a more prominent voice. The coalition's deputy director Leonard Lamkin explains, "People just saw it as kids being kids, but now we're beginning to see that the community support is there. Just as drunk driving came to be seen as a much more serious crime over the years, now the issue of allowing underage children to drink is being taken to the next level."

Parents may be less eager to provide drinking opportunities for their children if they knew the facts about early drinking and its lingering effect on young people. Around the country there are grassroots campaigns to discourage parents from allowing under-age drinking in their homes. In Ohio and Texas, local police departments, schools, and community programs have instituted a public service project called "Parents Who Host, Lose the Most: Don't be a Party to Teenage Drinking."

According to a poll conducted for the Ohio campaign, 37 per-cent of 1,381 parents and 46 percent of 874 teens surveyed said they were aware of other parents who host drinking parties. During the two-month period before the survey, 36 percent of the teens reported that they attended a party at which alcohol was served.

Parents living in Dallas who allow other people's children to drink at their homes now face stiffer consequences than ever before. Police departments throughout the state have a "zero tol-erance" policy for the offense, meaning that police officers are no longer allowed to issue parents a warning not to do it again. The Dallas campaign was inspired by a 1999 incident in which police issued 200 alcohol and curfew violations to teens at a single party. The high school student who organized that party received a year's probation and the adult who assisted him was sentenced to

90 days in jail and a $2,000 fine. Now parents face up to a year in prison and a $4,000 fine.

"In the old days, Officer Friendly would pour it out, give the kids a lecture and say, 'Don't let me catch you with this again,'" said Police Officer Darrell F. Fant, who is in charge of law enforcement for the Dallas campaign. "With zero tolerance, the individual discretion of the officer is taken away. We're going to file every case."

Chapter Four

Several destructive behaviors of underage drinkers would not be carried out if they were sober. Of those who commit crimes before they turn 18, 30 percent get into trouble while they are drunk.

The Unforeseen Consequences of Drinking

I n the summer of 1999, Gerald and Joan Coscia were looking forward to moving into their new $1.3-million home in Solebury Township, a quiet and affluent suburb north of Philadelphia. The home was nearly finished and soon the couple would be able to show off their new property to friends and family.

The Coscias did not suspect that other people had taken notice of their nearly finished home, situated on a secluded road. Young trespassers, who did not personally know the Coscias, decided the unoccupied house would be the perfect place to host an underage drinking party. The three 20-year-old men charged guests $5 for admission. With a fake I.D. they bought 12 large cases of beer. Marijuana and cocaine were also available to guests who heard about the party by word of mouth.

To get into the house, the young party planners kicked in the home's locked front door. At 7:30 P.M., guests began to arrive and enter after paying the $5 cover charge. Some left when they learned that the party organizers did not

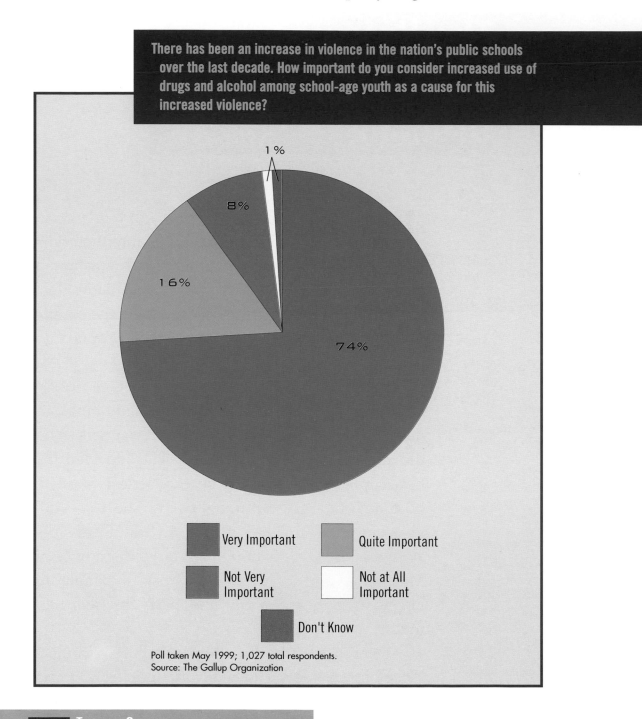

There has been an increase in violence in the nation's public schools over the last decade. How important do you consider increased use of drugs and alcohol among school-age youth as a cause for this increased violence?

1%

8%

16%

74%

Very Important

Quite Important

Not Very Important

Not at All Important

Don't Know

Poll taken May 1999; 1,027 total respondents.
Source: The Gallup Organization

know the people who owned the house. But many teenagers stayed and drank hundreds of beers. The party was still going strong at midnight when the drinking began to take its toll on the guests and the house.

One inebriated guest put his head, fist, elbow, foot, and a can of beer through a wall. Kitchen cabinets were pulled from the walls, and 17 large windows were shattered. Newly laid stone and hardwood floors were damaged and appliances pulled out of the wall. Beer was spilled everywhere and hundreds of cans scattered about. As if that were not bad enough, some of the partygoers urinated wherever they pleased, even though the home had five bathrooms.

When workmen discovered the vandalism the morning after, Police Officer Dan Boyle was dispatched to investigate. What he found was the worst case of vandalism he had seen in more than two decades. The bill to repair the damage climbed to $110,000. A quick investigation led police to the culprits. Boyle was surprised that he knew many of the "ordinary" kids who were at the party. A total of 34 young people eventually pleaded guilty to causing the damage, and 11 of them were given short prison terms and directed to pay compensation to the Coscias. The rest were given fines that they—and not their parents—were ordered to pay.

Residents of the area were stunned by the teenagers' destruction, including local district attorney Alan Rubenstein. "A large group of juveniles decide to go to a secluded home and drink beer," he said. "While that's wrong, it does not give me pause. It happens everywhere. It happens on a daily, on a nightly basis. What takes this beyond the norm is they decided to trash the place."

This account is extreme but illustrates what can occur when

teens do things they would almost never do sober. The U.S. Department of Justice reports a strong link between alcohol and crimes committed by young people. The agency says drinking was a factor in more than 27 percent of murders, 31 percent of rapes, 33 percent of crimes against property, and more than 37 percent of robberies committed by teenagers.

Of youths who commit crimes before the age of 18, 30 percent get into trouble while they are intoxicated. Victims of crime often suffer under similar circumstances. They may be taken advantage of because they have been drinking and appear to be easy marks. Half of the victims of campus crimes are college students who have been impaired by drugs or alcohol, according to the National Council on Alcohol and Drug Dependence.

Crime is but one unintended consequence of many involving underage drinking. Teens who drink may also find themselves coping with alcohol dependence, pregnancy and fetal alcohol syndrome, sexually transmitted diseases, sexual violence, depression, and suicidal thoughts. The Gallup Youth Survey has looked at the risky behavior of teens and has found that alcohol is often included in the mix. In 1990, researchers focused on whether teenagers know they can get in trouble if they drink, and discovered that the vast majority of young people do realize alcohol consumption can cause problems.

In that survey, 99 percent of the teenagers who participated said they know that pregnant women who consume alcohol risk having babies with birth defects. In addition, 95 percent of the teens said they know alcohol can be addictive and 85 percent said they regard alcoholism as a disease.

The 1990 survey also found that 82 percent of the respondents knew that prison inmates frequently had alcohol problems before they were sentenced. Also, 72 percent said they know women and men have different tolerances for alcohol, while 84 percent knew that people who drink are also likely to try drugs. On the subjects of alcohol addiction and drunken driving, 92 percent said they were aware that people who only drink wine and beer can become alcoholics, and 98 percent said they knew that even one or two drinks can impair a driver's abilities. A separate survey that year

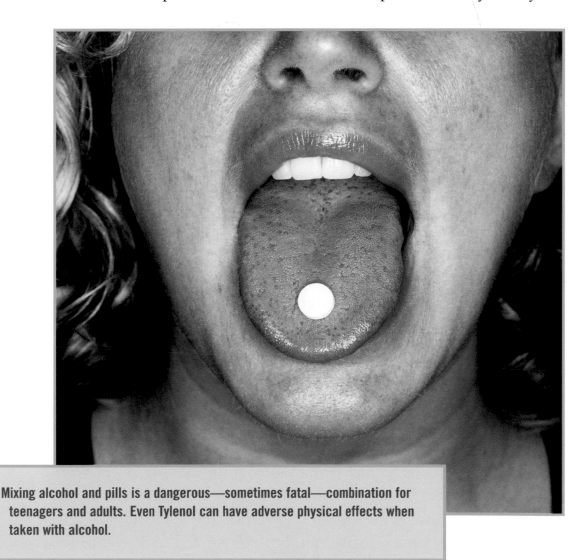

Mixing alcohol and pills is a dangerous—sometimes fatal—combination for teenagers and adults. Even Tylenol can have adverse physical effects when taken with alcohol.

found that 78 percent of the teen respondents believed drinking had a serious effect on American society.

Taking that first sip of alcohol is one of life's milestones. It may seem like a cool, grown-up thing to do at the time, but many teens will quickly become dependent on alcohol or move on to other forms of getting high, sometimes mixing alcohol with pills, which may turn out to be a deadly combination. Many young people do not realize that alcohol makes prescription drugs unpredictably more potent and potentially life threatening. When combined with alcohol, even Tylenol can damage the liver and have fatal effects on the body.

STDs, Pregnancy, and Fetal Alcohol Syndrome

Alcohol loosens inhibitions and dulls a person's judgment. For teens who are already thinking about sex, alcohol may prompt them to act on their impulses. This may result in them having sex without contraception, with pregnancy and exposure to sexually transmitted diseases like AIDS as possible consequences. Teenagers account for one-quarter of the 12 million new STD infections that are diagnosed each year.

A recent report released by the National Center on Addiction and Substance Abuse at Columbia University in New York found that 63 percent of teens who drink engage in sex. The study also revealed that young people aged 14 and under were twice as likely to have sexual intercourse if they drank while 15-year-olds were seven times as likely to have intercourse if they drank. They were also more likely to have sex with multiple partners. Another study, organized by the Kaiser Family Foundation of Menlo Park, California, found that nearly one out of five 13- to 19-year-olds were drinking before they had their first sexual experience.

One of the major consequences facing teenagers who engage in unprotected sexual intercourse is unplanned pregnancies. According to the Alan Guttmacher Institute, which studies adolescent sexual issues, there were about 880,000 pregnancies among teenage girls between the ages of 15 and 19 in 1996. Of those pregnant teens, 35 percent decided to have an abortion.

For those who keep their babies, life changes dramatically. Consuelo Cruz, a 17-year-old from Santa Fe, New Mexico, found that out when she gave birth to her son, Nicholas, in 1999. "I was scared and worried about what my friends and family would think," she told a reporter. "My aspects of life have definitely

Because alcohol loosens inhibitions, many teenage drinkers engage in unplanned sex. As a result, this group faces high rates of sexually transmitted diseases and unplanned pregnancies.

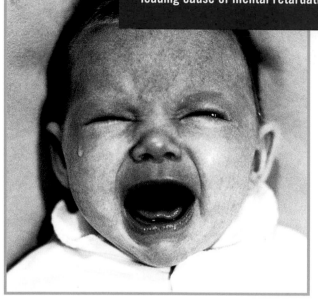

changed. No more partying; no more school. Now I have to think about somebody before I can think about myself. You have to grow up really fast. If you are not ready for that, then you should be more careful in the choices you make." Many teens who get pregnant don't even plan on having sex, until drinking alcohol impairs their judgment. In a 1990 study in the journal *Adolescence*, one-third of the 14- to 21-year-olds who became pregnant said they had been drinking when they conceived.

Should teenage mothers continue to drink, they may face another consequence—fetal alcohol syndrome, or FAS. While being pregnant can ruin a teenager's plans for college and career, it can also leave dire consequences for the baby when the mother drinks during her pregnancy. Expectant mothers who drink alcohol are more likely to miscarry than those who do not drink, no matter what their age. When they carry their babies to term, the infants may also weigh less than most babies.

Since 1981, every bottle of alcohol sold in the United States has carried on its label a warning to women: "According to the Surgeon General, women should not drink alcoholic beverages during pregnancy because of the risks of birth defects." While the warning has discouraged maternal drinking, FAS remains the most common and preventable birth defect in the United States. As recently as 1995, 15 percent of pregnant women were still drinking despite the known dangers to their unborn children.

FAS is the leading known cause of mental retardation. Each year between 5,000 and 10,000 babies are born with below-average intelligence because their mothers drank during pregnancy. Women who average two drinks a day will have babies that weigh less and have more intellectual problems than the babies of women who don't drink at all. If they have an average of three drinks a day, it is virtually certain that their babies will suffer from FAS.

FAS babies share certain facial features. Small heads and eyes, short noses, and thin lips set these babies apart from other infants. These babies may also develop seizures caused by their dependence on alcohol. They may also experience poor reflexes, short attention spans, difficulty sleeping, trouble learning, and an inability to gain weight. Finally, they may suffer from problems with their heart, joints, and bladder. There is no cure for FAS and the problems that accompany it stay with a person throughout his or her life. That's a pretty high price to pay for a short period of drinking.

Teresa Kellerman, adoptive mother of a son born with FAS and executive director of the FAS Community Resource Center in Tucson, Arizona, puts a human face on this sad health condition. In 1995 she described what life was like for her 18-year-old son John, who was born with what she describes as a "life-long hangover." At the time of her story, he was incapable of driving a car, was having a difficult time in school, and didn't have friends. She wrote:

> John is not as bright, not as tall, not as good-looking as other teens his age. He has a hard time learning the rules of life, and when he learns them, he has a hard time remembering them. His behavior and mannerisms seem inappropriate to most people, and while he desires to be close to people and has a friendly and out-going personality, others are put off and maybe repulsed, and then shy away from him.

Rape and Suicide

Alcohol plays a role in many date rapes and sexual assaults affecting teenagers and college students. A study written in 2002 by the National Institute on Alcohol Abuse and Alcoholism reported that drinking plays a role in 70,000 cases of sexual assaults or date rapes on college campuses a year.

Even elite institutions of higher learning like the Air Force Academy in Colorado Springs, Colorado, where some of the brightest young men and women in the country train to be commissioned officers in the U.S. Air Force, have been touched by drinking-related sex scandals. In March 2003 the Air Force Academy was in the middle of investigating 56 allegations of rape and sexual assault. That month, Air Force Secretary James Roche stated during a congressional hearing that "there are probably a hundred more [cases of rape and sexual assault] that we do not see." In an e-mail to her peers, one female cadet who said her report of a rape had been ignored by her superiors wrote: "Rape has been a dirty secret at the [academy] for over 20 years. . . . [L]eaders know about what goes on, but won't do anything that may hurt the academy's reputation." In about half of the incidents reported at the Air Force Academy, drinking was said to have played a role. One 18-year-old female testified that before she was accosted she had consumed six glasses of tequila, which put her into a semi-conscious state.

Matt James, vice president of the Kaiser Family Foundation,

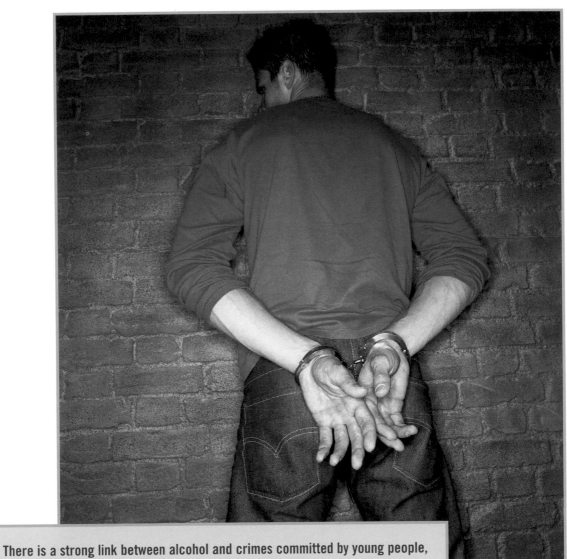

There is a strong link between alcohol and crimes committed by young people, one of which is rape. Alcohol is reported to play a role in thousands of date rapes every year.

believes that statistics show a relationship between drinking and sexual recklessness that is too strong to ignore. Based on information collected in conjunction with the Centers for Disease Control and Prevention, the Kaiser researchers reported that one out of five people between the ages of 13 and 19 were drinking the first time they had sex. Also, out of a group of 14- to 22-year-old males, only 22 percent of those who used drugs or alcohol wore condoms the last time they had sex. In contrast, 65 percent of those not using any substances wore condoms the last time they had sex.

"This ought to be a wake-up call for people who are involved in the lives of young people," James said of the alarming numbers. "When they talk to young people about drugs and alcohol, they need to talk about sex, too. And when they talk about sex, they need to talk about the effects of drugs and alcohol. Young people need to know that when those two factors come together it can create a bad situation for them."

Teenage suicide is a phenomenon typically brought on by depression and other forms of mental illness. One factor common to depression as well as most suicides among young people is the abuse of drugs or alcohol. "Analyses of data for adolescents . . . document a close association between substances and suicide," said a 1989 report on teenage suicide prepared by the U.S. Alcohol, Drug Abuse and Mental Health Administration.

The study tracked cases involving young suicide victims over a period of 10 years and concluded that youths who abused drugs and alcohol were up to eight times more likely to kill themselves than youths who didn't drink or take drugs. The study found "frequent use of nonprescription drugs or alcohol" among 70 percent of the 20 teenagers who committed suicide in the Louisville, Kentucky, area between 1980 and 1983. Almost half the suicide victims between the ages of 15 and 19 in Erie County, New York, had alcohol in their blood. The study also found that in San Diego, California, 75 percent of young suicide victims had abused substances, and that each young victim consumed drugs or alcohol as many as five times just prior to their deaths.

Alcohol and drugs often help make a bad problem worse. Alcohol often has a depressive effect on the brain, which means it can make depressed people feel even worse about themselves. Drinking also helps alter judgment, and interferes with the ability to assess risk, make smart choices, and think of solutions to problems.

Chapter Five

The aftermath of a car wreck involving alcohol, an all-too-familiar scene for police and rescue workers. Teens are among the thousands of motorists cited for drinking and driving every year.

Too Young to Die: Teenage Drinking and Driving

After graduating from Quakertown High School in Pennsylvania, Allison Reboratti was not sure about what she wanted to do with her life. She took one part-time job after another as she struggled with that question. By the time she was 19, though, she thought she had figured it out. She planned to spend the next year volunteering; then she would go to art school to hone her natural talents for drawing, painting, and sculpting.

As a volunteer, she would work with a national service group called Ameri-Corp. As an incentive for signing up she was to receive a $5,000 voucher she could use for art school. Only one small detail was yet to be determined—whether she would work in an Ameri-Corp program in North Carolina or California.

On May 8, 2001, a letter was delivered telling her the details of her assignment. While the letter sat at home unopened, the dark-haired teenager was out with her friend, Steven Filipak, an 18-year-old from near-by Emmaus and employee at an automotive supply store. That afternoon Steven had driven the couple to the city of Allentown, where they ran some errands and visited a friend who was having a party. At the friend's house, Steven began drinking and passed out. When he woke up hours later, he told Allison he felt sober enough to drive.

The two teenagers climbed into Steven's gold 1977 Ford Granada for the ride home. Neither occupant of the car buckled their seat belts as Steven drove off, well into the early morning hours of May 9. The night was clear and Allison was nearly home when the car entered a dark, two-lane stretch of road. The speed limit was 40 miles per hour but the Granada was traveling at speeds approaching 70. Steven had a problem with driving reck-lessly and had already been issued several warnings by local police. Steven lost control of the car. The Granada spun counter-clockwise as it left the road and came to a stop after the passenger side struck a sign post, a fence, and an evergreen tree.

When the paramedics arrived they found Allison dead, laying across Steven's lap. Breathing but unconscious, Steven was taken to Lehigh Valley Hospital in Allentown where doctors determined that he had broken bones and suffered brain damage, which would leave him unable to remember the accident or much of any-thing else.

Even with such extensive injuries that kept him in the hospital for five months, Steven faced criminal charges in Allison's death. He pleaded guilty to homicide and aggravated assault by vehicle, as well as involuntary manslaughter. A judge gave Steven a prison sentence of two and a half to five years, but allowed him to serve his sentence as an inpatient at a brain injury foundation.

Prosecuting attorney John S. Benson said Steven's case showed the worst that can happen when an inebriated teen gets behind the wheel. "It's a study of what can go wrong by drinking and driving," he said. "Here, a wonderfully gifted 19-year-old woman is dead, and all she did was get into the car that night. People have to understand that if you drink and drive this is going to happen."

As a result of the brain damage he suffered, Steven has difficulty comprehending that lesson. His attorney, Christopher Spadoni, said Steven only knows he caused Allison's death because other people have told him about it.

Unlike Steven, Casey McCary Bloom will never be able to forget

Although the odds of an intoxicated driver being stopped are less than 1 in 1,000 driving trips, Driving While Intoxicated (DWI)—also called Driving Under the Influence (DUI)—is the most common crime committed in the United States.

his nightmare that ended in a wrongful death. Casey and his college friends were enjoying their summer break at his parent's beach house. They lazed on the beach, drank beer, danced, and stayed up until 1 A.M. enjoying their freedom. The vacation was going smoothly until they decided to gas up the truck at an all-night convenience store and buy cigarettes. They found a place open two miles away and headed back to the beach house with their purchases.

Casey was driving the truck when it struck another car that he failed to see. One of the car's four passengers, 17-year-old Donn'elle McGraw, died instantly. Mark Weber, who had been sitting in the back of the car with Donn'elle, was critically injured. The other person injured in the crash was Casey's friend, who was sent through the windshield of the truck.

"I will never forget the screaming and crying that I heard that night," Casey wrote in an essay entitled "Drunk Driving Brings a Lifetime of Pain," which he composed while in prison. "When the police arrived, I was questioned, handcuffed and arrested." Casey was charged with two felonies — manslaughter while driving under the influence and causing serious bodily injury while driving under the influence. He was convicted of both charges and is serving 21 years in prison. In his mind, he is serving a life sentence. He wrote: "But no physical punishment I receive will compare to the emotional punishment I have been going through and will go through for the rest of my life."

According to a Gallup Youth Survey conducted in 2000, 5 percent of teenagers admit to having driven a car after consuming alcohol. Thirteen percent of the respondents said they had been a passenger in a car driven by someone who had recently been drinking. The number of teens that report making these kinds of choices has been declining since 1984, when 14 percent of teens said they had driven after drinking and 36 percent had ridden with a driver who had been drinking. Even with the decline, drinking and driving is still a major killer, with more people killed by drunken drivers than by guns.

Drunk Driving and the Law

The first laws against drunken driving coincided with the advent of the first automobiles. Henry Ford, founder of the Ford Motor Company and developer of the first mass-produced American car, sensed how dangerous the combination of drinking and driving could be. "Booze had to go when modern industry and the motor car came in," he said. New York State made drunken driving a crime in 1910, and California and other states soon outlawed the practice as well. The laws, however, were difficult to enforce for many decades because policemen had no definitive tests to prove that someone was drunk. Up until the early 1950s, they could only testify on what they observed with their own eyes— whether someone exhibited slurred speech, was unsteady walking, or smelled of alcohol—to convince a judge or jury.

Proving someone's level of intoxication became a simple matter when Dr. Robert Borkenstein, a member of the Indiana State Police, invented the Breathalyzer machine in the 1950s. The device assesses blood-alcohol concentration (BAC) levels, which are now crucial pieces of evidence in courts of law.

At one time, the legal limit for BAC had varied from state to state, but in recent years, all states have lowered it from 0.10 percent to 0.08 percent. In other words, if there are 0.08 grams or more of alcohol present in 100 milliliters of someone's blood, the driver is regarded as intoxicated. The state senates lowered the level to

An accident memorial site demands justice for the drunk driver responsible for killing a motorist. Like adult offenders, teenagers who cause drunken driving deaths may be charged with manslaughter or homicide by vehicle.

comply with a federal law signed in 2000 by President Bill Clinton, which required the .08 percent BAC in order for states to qualify for highway construction and repair subsidies.

The change in the law was supported by most Americans, according to a poll conducted by the Gallup Organization. In the year in which President Clinton signed the law, 72 percent of respondents supported lowering the BAC as an initiative to reduce drinking and driving. Although the poll was not part of the

Gallup Youth Survey, the Gallup Organization did include some young people in the sampling. Among the 1,002 people contacted for the poll were respondents who were 16 and 17 years old.

How does alcohol impair driving skills? Reaction time is critical to operating a vehicle safely. At a moment's notice one must react to stopping school buses, passing ambulances, children riding bicycles, and other motorists who suddenly pull out into traffic. Add alcohol to the mix, and reaction time is slowed, reflexes are dulled, attention wanes, and judgment decreases. Worst of all, an impaired driver is often the last to realize that he or she is not fit to drive.

The typical drunk driver is a white male who is proud of his driving skills and ability to hold his liquor. He is most likely to be involved in a fatal one-car accident at night while driving in the suburbs, according to the National Commission Against Drunk Driving. While adults are more likely to drive while intoxicated than teenagers, it is the younger, less experienced drivers who are more likely to wind up dead. "While fewer young drivers drink, those who do are more dangerous drivers and are significantly overrepresented among traffic fatalities," says James B. Jacobs, director of the Center for Research in Crime and Justice at New York University. This discrepancy is explained by the fact that younger drivers are less experienced at judging how far away other vehicles are and at what speed they are traveling.

In 1999, police cited 1.5 million motorists for drinking and driving, making DUI the most common crime in the United States. The majority of those stopped by police had no previous arrests. Of course, that does not mean that many of these individuals never drove while intoxicated before. In fact, the true odds of being arrested for DUI are less than 1 in 1,000 trips of driving.

Under the law, teenagers who are stopped for drunken driving are treated differently than adults. Because it is illegal for teenagers to drink alcohol, they can be cited for underage drinking even if they are not legally drunk. Thus, any recorded BAC level can put them in danger of having their driver's license suspended and paying a fine. First-time offenders are treated less harshly than those with previous DUI arrests, who may face jail time and community service. If the teenager driver causes a death, he or she may be tried for manslaughter, which is defined as the killing of another person without express malice. A more serious charge is homicide by vehicle, in which prosecutors allege the driver flagrantly violated the laws against drinking and driving.

Mothers Against Drunk Driving

As Ricardo Martinez, head of the National Highway Traffic Safety Administration, points out, a car can wipe out an entire family faster than a machine gun. In recent years state legislators have acknowledged how serious the drunk driving problem is by enacting tough laws that carry stiff sentences for violators. One organization that helped elevate the public consciousness about drinking and driving is MADD, which stands for Mothers Against Drunk Driving.

MADD was begun in 1980 by a group of mothers from California. They were outraged at the death of a 13-year-old girl by a drunken driver who was a repeat offender. MADD now has a powerful nationwide presence, with more than 2 million members in 624 chapters. Its lobbying efforts have been largely responsible for cutting the number of deaths from drinking and driving from 28,000 in 1980 to about 16,000 in 2000. In addition, the group has helped convince legislators to pass 2,500 laws clamping down on drunken drivers.

Through MADD's efforts, much of the American public no longer regards driving drunk as a minor nuisance or a laughable situation. MADD's lobbying was a key factor in raising the minimum drinking age to 21 in the 1980s. Also, the legislation for a consistent minimum drinking age across the United States ended the risky practice of teens driving out of state to legally obtain liquor.

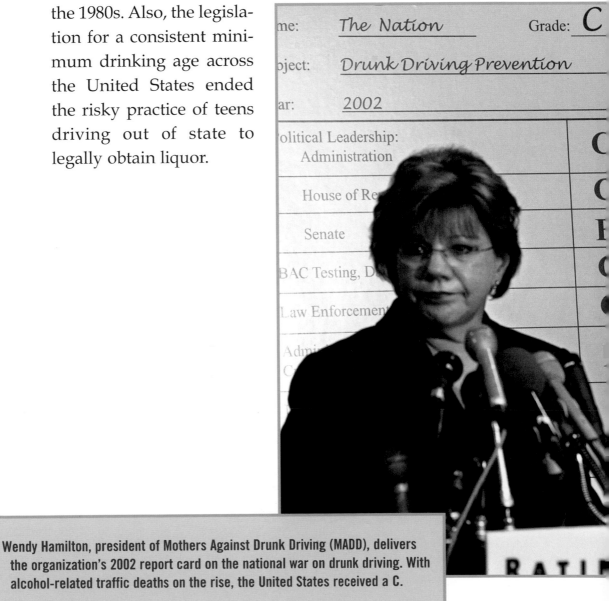

Wendy Hamilton, president of Mothers Against Drunk Driving (MADD), delivers the organization's 2002 report card on the national war on drunk driving. With alcohol-related traffic deaths on the rise, the United States received a C.

Chapter Six

While they attend college, young people are at risk of the most dangers associated with drinking. Consequences range from poor academic performance to alcohol poisoning and date rape.

College and the Party Lifestyle

Jeffrey Blume studies political science at George Washington University in Washington, D.C. After observing the heavy drinking lifestyle of some of his fellow students, he wonders why they profess to be academically involved at all. In a May 2003 column for the *Philadelphia Inquirer*, Blume wrote, "Adults cannot imagine how much a normal college student drinks on a typical weekend night, and sometimes on weekdays. I've seen guys put away an average of 10 or 12 alcoholic beverages."

According to Blume, it is a rare weekend when he doesn't hear about a freshman being hospitalized for alcohol poisoning. The 22-year-old student admitted having his first drink at 16, when he said it was easy to get beer whenever he wanted it. "[W]e knew which beer distributorships were willing to sell to underage kids," he wrote. Pennsylvania's government-owned liquor store system "made liquor harder to come by, but it, too, often was available," he added. "Someone's older

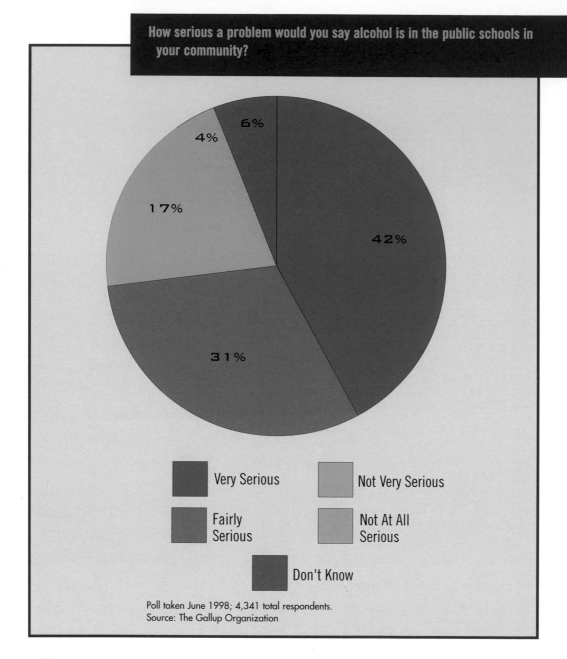

How serious a problem would you say alcohol is in the public schools in your community?

6%

4%

17%

42%

31%

Very Serious

Not Very Serious

Fairly Serious

Not At All Serious

Don't Know

Poll taken June 1998; 4,341 total respondents.
Source: The Gallup Organization

sibling sometimes was willing to buy liquor for us, or a friend's parent had a well-stocked liquor cabinet. A bottle or two wouldn't be missed."

Blume maintains that young people should learn how to drink while in high school and under the watchful eyes of their parents before they come to college and totally lose control. He said his fellow college students drink out of rebellion against the contradictions that allow 18-year-olds to register for the draft, to vote, and face the death penalty but deny them the right to celebrate good times with alcohol.

Regardless of whether Blume's ideas of supervised drinking have merit, there is no question that binge drinking on college campuses—drinking four or five alcoholic beverages in a short period of time—is a serious problem. In fact, college students spend more money on alcohol than they do on soft drinks, milk, juice, tea, coffee, and textbooks combined. A 1991 study by the Substance Abuse and Mental Health Services Administration estimated that

Some college students who are uninterested in drinking and the party life have pushed their schools to promote more alcohol-free activities.

students spent $5.5 billion annually on alcohol. The amount of drinking suggested by that total is a source of headaches for college administrators who must deal with the riots, vandalism, and health issues resulting from student drinking.

The 1991 study also found that beer is the much-preferred beverage of choice by college students. The study estimated that college students drink 4 billion cans of beer a year—up to 430

ALCOHOL'S GREATEST MYTHS

Many teens hear things about alcohol that aren't true from friends who are trying to talk them into drinking. These myths about alcohol may seem credible but are not, according to Mothers Against Drunk Driving.

Myth: Beer is harmless.
Fact: Beer contains alcohol, which can damage the heart, liver, and stomach.

Myth: Strong coffee or a cold shower can speed up sobriety.
Fact: Once someone is drunk, his or her body needs time to rid itself of the alcohol. There is no proven way to speed up this process.

Myth: Drinking is sexy.
Fact: Alcohol can make people act on their sexual impulses, but it also impairs sexual functioning. Drinking limits good judgment, making some people do things they would never do sober—like assault a date and engage in unprotected intercourse.

Myth: A hangover is the worst that can happen.
Fact: Hangovers are an inconvenience, but nothing at all compared to dying in an accident, blacking out, or suffering alcohol poisoning.

Myth: Drinking is a lot safer than taking drugs.
Fact: More than six times the number of people killed by cocaine, heroin, and other illegal drugs combined are killed by alcohol.

million gallons of beer. This is enough for each college in the United States to fill an Olympic-size pool.

Alcohol and College Sports

Binge drinking is more popular with college-age sports fans than non-sports fans, according to a 2002 survey by the Harvard School of Public Health. There were 14,000 college students surveyed, and of those who drank, 53 percent of the sports fans were binge drinkers. In contrast, only 41 percent of male and 37 percent

Myth: Drinking only harms the drinker.
Fact: The behavior of every person who drinks excessively or illegally affects at least four other people, according to MADD. This may include mothers, fathers, brothers, and sisters.

Myth: Friends with drinking problems are best left alone.
Fact: A good friend will not ignore someone else's drinking problem. Instead, he or she will share observations about the person's behavior in hopes of raising awareness about the problem.

Myth: Everybody reacts the same to alcohol.
Fact: There are big differences in the way people react to alcohol. Some drinkers become happy, others cry easily. Body size, sex, and genetics are a few of the factors that can make one person's drinking experience different from another's.

Myth: Mixing liquor can get someone drunk quicker.
Fact: Alternating between wine, liquor, and beer won't affect intoxication levels. The key is how much total alcohol ends up in the bloodstream.

of female non-sports fans said they binged.

Many college sports programs expand their budgets by accepting money for sponsorships from beer companies, which some people regard as a corrupting influence on young people. More typically, beer companies pay to advertise during televised college events, despite the fact that most of the students who attend games or view them on TV at home are not old enough to legally drink. At some college stadiums, beer is available for sale from vendors.

Drunken college students may become violent or destructive after football games. In 1998, thousands of Michigan State University students damaged public property and started fires during one football weekend. Cars were overturned and police in riot gear had to be called in to restore order. Many of the rioters were under the influence of alcohol. A similar incident took place at Ohio State University in November 2002, when the Buckeyes battled rival Michigan State. Some young fans were already drunk at 8 A.M. on the day of the big game. When the Buckeyes won the game, fans rushed the field. Later that night, when the bars shut down, more than 100 fires were set. Throughout the campus in Columbus, cars were overturned and windows smashed.

The National Collegiate Athletic Association, the organization responsible for overseeing college sports, has reacted to this controversy. In April 2003 the NCAA refused to let Miller Brewing Company air a commercial during the broadcast of the Final Four championship tournament, college basketball's premier sporting event. The Miller ad that was taken off the air was to feature two busty women fighting—and ripping each other's clothes off—as they argued over whether the beer "tastes great" or is "less filling." Explaining the decision, NCAA President Myles Brand said,

"There has to be some sense of decorum in commercials."

The NCAA has enacted other restrictions on alcohol advertising. For example, it decided to prohibit hard liquor from being advertised during championship games and to restrict beer and wine advertising to 14 percent of game-program content. Now, televised games can have only 60 seconds of beer and wine advertising per hour.

Brand sees no need for further restrictions. "If you just take the beer commercials out of college sports media, I'm not sure what effect that will have because beer commercials appear in many, many other places," he said. Others disagree, like Hodding Carter III, president of the service group the Knight Foundation: "The problem is when you rest your economic viability on the money that television gives you, TV will say, 'Where do you think we get *our* money from?'"

While serving as secretary of Health and Human Services in the Clinton administration, Donna E. Shalala suggested NCAA officials "completely, absolutely and forever" disassociate themselves from alcohol. Since she became president of the University of Miami in 2000, that course of action has been more difficult than it seemed at first, though she and other presidents still wish to hold colleges up to a high standard. "I don't think the problem is the beer companies," she said. "The problem is us. We've got to decide what's appropriate for our college campuses."

The federally funded Task Force on College Drinking reported that each year 1,400 college students die from accidents in which alcohol is a contributing factor. It also found that 70,000 cases of sexual assault or date rape are attributable to drinking, as are 500,000 injuries. Among high school students, drinking also has adverse effects on classroom practices. A Gallup Youth Survey conducted in

2003 on cheating in the classroom found that 66 percent of teenagers who said they drink admitted to cheating on tests.

Binge Drinking

Bloomington, Indiana, is best known as the home of the 38,000-student campus of Indiana University. The university has a highly regarded reputation in sciences, music, business, education, journalism, and the arts. Its administrators are less pleased about one particular fact regarding the school: it was listed as the No. 1 party school in the 2002 *Princeton Review*. The book ranks 345 schools according to a number of criteria, with "party" rankings based on student answers to questions on the presence of hard liquor, significance of fraternity and sorority life on campus, and lack of time spent studying.

According to *Time* magazine, six Indiana University fraternities have lost their charters since January 2001 because of alcohol violations. In addition, the number of Indiana students arrested for underage drinking has quadrupled since 1998. Alcohol has claimed the lives of several students, including the 2001 death of 19-year-old Seth Korona. The young student had only been on the Bloomington campus a month when he was fatally injured at a fraternity party. Korona suffered a fractured skull when he fell and hit his head on a doorframe while attempting to do a keg stand, a maneuver that involves performing a handstand over a beer keg while drinking from its tap.

Last year, 52 percent of students at Indiana University described themselves as binge drinkers. There are six off-campus bars that cater to thirsty students. A bar game called Bladder Busters encourages students to drink all they can for 50-cent drinks. "We all got fake IDs the second we joined the sorority," said Indiana University student Krissy Selleck. Fellow student Will Loy set up his class roster to facilitate his recreational drinking. By taking classes later in the day, he found he could study at noon and still maintain a decent grade point average. And he could do that while staying up until 3 A.M., bar hopping and consuming as many as 12 drinks per night.

Peer pressure to drink at college is a universal problem that extends beyond the American college circuit. Shannon Belmore, a journalism student at Ryerson Polytechnic University in Toronto, Ontario, recalled what it was like during FROSH week, when new freshmen arrive on campus. "For many, FROSH week is the beginning of the everlasting party that their newfound freedom will provide," she wrote. "For others, like myself, FROSH week means trying to fit in as a non-drinker." Belmore observed that 7 out of 10 activities scheduled during that first week on campus involved drinking. Having been raised in an alcoholic family, she found the free-flow of alcohol to be a scary situation. She wrote:

> I am not against drinking in moderation, nor do I see any problems in drinking socially. The problem arises, however, when students begin to feel that the only way to have fun or to fit in at social events is to drink. . . . It would be nice if more people would recognize that not everyone at university drinks, and that more campus activities should be organized for non-drinkers.

About 44 percent of college students binge drink, according to the Harvard School of Public Health College Alcohol Study. About half of them begin binge drinking in high school and continue the behavior into their college years. College students are more likely to drink to excess than young adults who don't go to college. Of all campus groups, athletes have the highest rate of binging—even higher than fraternity members, reports the *Journal of American College Health*.

"College binge drinking is a major public health issue and a source of numerous problems for institutions of higher learning," said Dr. Richard Yoast, director of A Matter of Degree, the American Medical Association's organization dedicated to working with universities to stem alcohol abuse. Studies conducted by A Matter of Degree showed that 95 percent of the parents believed that binge drinking was a "serious threat to their children."

Alternatives to Drinking

Keg parties at fraternities have been a tradition at colleges for many decades, but that is now changing. A combination of deaths, lawsuits, higher insurance premiums, and a backlash against alcohol use have led to a new type of fraternity—one that is alcohol-free. First recommended in 1997 by the National Interfraternity Council, no-alcohol-allowed fraternities are growing in number across the country.

A sober Greek life seemed unappealing to some at first, but the idea has been catching on as fraternity brothers find that their houses have become quieter and cleaner and recruiting new members has not been a problem. Said Dan Kline, a member of the Acacia fraternity at Iowa State University, "I think it is a reflection on students nowadays that they want to come to school to study and meet friends rather than just drink."

In addition to a changing fraternity culture, many colleges are also taking steps to reduce the number of drinkers on their campuses. The Robert Wood Johnson Foundation, a Princeton-based philanthropic organization dedicated to health care, has coordinated with A Matter of Degree to launch an $8.6 million, seven-year program to reduce high-risk drinking among college students at 10 universities.

The universities participating in the program are working to beef up their own alcohol policies. They are also forming partnerships with their neighboring communities to enforce underage drinking laws. At the University of Wisconsin, the coalition is seeking to limit late-night drink specials at off-campus bars. Other plans by the university and the city government in Madison include notifying parents of underage drinking violations, addressing the dangers of house parties, and clarifying and publicizing its expectations of student conduct. Florida State has banned alcohol advertising on campus, provides substance-free housing, and has organized alcohol-free activities on Thursdays, typically a bar night off campus.

Student groups have also gotten involved in efforts to curb drinking. Those groups include SADD (Students Against Destructive Decisions) and BACCHUS (Boosting Alcohol Consciousness Concerning the Health of University Students).

Fraternity members enjoy an obstacle course during an alcohol-free activity. In 1997 the National Interfraternity Council recommended that universities begin establishing no-alcohol-allowed fraternities on their campuses.

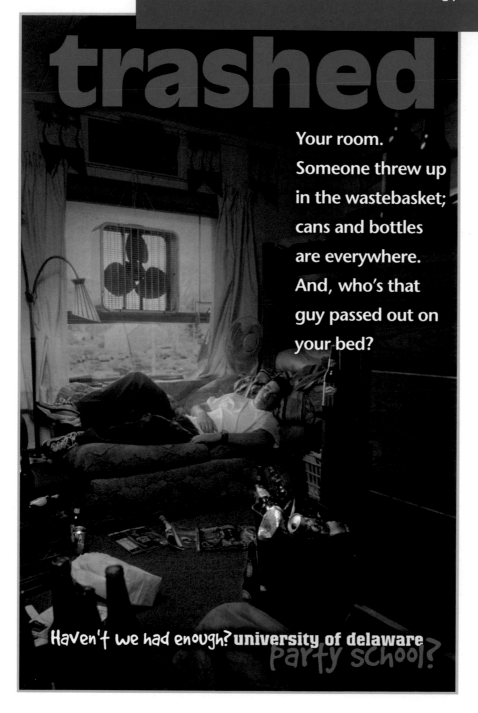

SADD was originally known as Students Against Drunk Driving. It was the brainchild of Robert Anastas, a high school teacher, and 15 students. In 1981, they founded the organization at Wayland High School in Massachusetts after two hockey players were killed in separate drunken driving incidents in the same month. SADD now has thousands of chapters in middle schools, high schools, and colleges where peers share anti-drinking messages with one another. Like SADD, but restricted to the university level, BACCHUS is a student-to-student program that encourages sensible decision-making and alcohol abuse prevention. There are chapters on most American college campuses.

A radical new approach to curbing college drinking is being tried at 30 college campuses around the country, including the state universities of Arizona, North Carolina, Oregon, and Missouri, as well as Rutgers University in New Jersey and 23 campuses of the University of California system. It is called "social norming" and its objective is not to scare students about the dangers of drinking but to promote the fact that many college students don't drink, don't binge, don't kill themselves, and don't drive drunk.

Michael Haines, a substance abuse expert at Northern Illinois University, is one of the leaders of the social norming movement. He believes that college authorities are mistaken in playing up incidences of drinking that occur on campuses. "The simple norm is that most students are drinking moderately, if at all, and are not harming anyone, and they'll mature into effective, capable people," Haines said. Campuses participating in the social norming program ask their students for data on their drinking habits and other risky behaviors, then report the results on bumper stickers, signs, and posters.

Chapter Seven

Many teenagers openly forsake the drug and alcohol lifestyle. Among this group are punk-rock enthusiasts known as straight-edgers, who since the early 1980s have spoken out against using alcohol, cigarettes, and other drugs.

"I've Got Better Things to Do"

In 1980, a Washington, D.C.–based punk band called Minor Threat made its reputation not by exhorting its fans to get high or drunk, but by admonishing them to stay away from drugs and alcohol. One of the group's most popular songs was "I've Got the Straight Edge." The song's lyrics, written by frontman Ian MacKaye, contains these words:

> I'm a person just like you
> But I've got better things to do
> Than sit around and smoke dope
> 'Cause I know I can cope
> Laugh at the thought of eating ludes
> Laugh at the thought of sniffing glue
> Always gonna keep in touch
> Never want to use a crutch
> I've got the straight edge

The group's fans, who became known as "straight-edgers," took up a lifestyle marked by what they would not do: smoke tobacco, take drugs, or drink alcohol. As a way of identifying themselves, straight-edgers marked the backs of their hands—either with marker or a permanent tattoo—with a black X. They had adopted the symbol from the nightclub bouncers, who originally used the X to identify underage concertgoers prohibited from buying alcohol. Eventually, "sXe" became the official straight-edge logo.

The straight-edge movement had its dark side. In the 1990s, straight-edgers developed a violent reputation for confronting young people who did not agree with their ideas about substance abuse. However, according to the Long Island, New York, newspaper *Newsday*, the straight-edge movement has made a positive comeback in recent years, with a new generation of young people promoting nonviolent issues like racial diversity, environmentalism, and pacifism. This group is using the Internet to promote its message of living without tobacco, drugs, and alcohol.

Monika Seitz of Columbus, Ohio, was only four years old when Minor Threat first performed the songs for which they are best known. Seitz, 24, says she has had only one beer in her life and perhaps two cigarettes since graduating from high school. She explains that rather than being a homogeneous, militant group as some have portrayed it, straight-edgers come from all walks of life, and each is free to his or her own approach to the drug-free lifestyle. Wheaton College in Norton, Massachusetts, has a dormitory with a straight-edge theme known as "X House." Wheaton senior Geoff Bickford, an X House resident, says he enjoys living there because it offers him a refuge from the average college town activities of drinking and getting high.

A large group of teenagers—including those who are not avowed stright-edgers—do not have respect for adults who drink. A Gallup Youth Survey conducted in 1996 interviewed 501 teenagers about behaviors they respected in adults. Only one teen in four said they thought adults who drank wine were sophisti-cated and admirable. Adults who drink beer fared even more poorly; only 12 percent of the teenagers respected beer-drinking adults.

Whether the straight-edge movement is here to stay isn't clear. Fad or not, straight-edgers are among the 34 percent of people who say they abstain from drinking alcohol. Some sober groups, like Mormons, Pentecostals, Baptists, and Muslims, do so for reli-gious reasons, while others abstain for health reasons. Abstainers also include recovering alcoholics and some children of alco-holics. Geography may be an influence in the drinking practices of some American communities: people who live in the South in rural Protestant communities are more likely to abstain from alco-hol than people living in any other part of the United States, for example. Ethnic groups also have different abstention rates: Caucasian men and women have the lowest abstention rates of all, while Asian American men and women have the highest rates, according to the National Institute on Alcohol Abuse and Alcoholism.

Alcohol Abuse in the Family

If a parent abuses alcohol or drugs, it is not unusual to see the pattern repeated with a child. About a quarter of children with alcoholic parents will grow up to be alcoholics or drug abusers, according to the American Academy of Children and Adolescent Psychiatry.

Jack Osbourne, teenage son of heavy metal rocker Ozzy Osbourne, briefly fell into a family pattern of drug abuse, and checked himself into a substance abuse clinic in April 2003. As fans of MTV's reality series *The Osbournes* know, Ozzy has a long

history of abusing drugs and alcohol. Said Jack Osbourne: "I got caught up in my new lifestyle and got carried away with drugs and alcohol. Once I realized this, I voluntarily checked myself into a detox facility for my own health and well-being."

While no two people are alike, there are certain commonly recognized signs pointing to a person's dependence on alcohol. These signs are the same for adults and teenagers:

Regularly getting drunk.
Refusing to admit to the amount of alcohol he or she consumed.
Spending more time alone getting drunk.
No longer participating in favorite sports or extracurricular activities, not doing homework, and avoiding friends who don't drink.
Sneaking alcohol from parents and planning ahead to get drunk.
Being hung over often and forgetting things said or done during a drinking session.
Talking about drinking, driving while drinking, and being stopped by the police.

Sometimes the only way to help other people realize the harm that drinking is doing is to talk to them about their alcohol problem. This may seem like an unpleasant thing to do, but it may be the last solution to helping a friend avoid permanent injury or even death. A 1996 Gallup Youth Survey found that troubled teens will often turn to their friends for assistance when they need help making important decisions. A total of 45 percent of the respondents said they often try to sort out right from wrong with their friends, while an additional 37 percent of the young people who responded to the survey said they sometimes turn to their friends for help.

The Center for Health Communication of the Harvard School of Public Health recommends speaking to the friend when he or she is sober. A good time is before school. Making accusations is a bad idea, but sharing observations about what he or she has done while under the influence of alcohol — without casting blame — is a good way to address the topic. It is also important to make it clear that you or another friend are willing to help. Someone with an alcohol problem may get angry, deny the problem, or defend his or her reasons for drinking. These reactions are all common and should be anticipated.

A great way to show that your intentions are positive is to find out where help is available, and promise to accompany the friend on the first visit. The friend needs to know that loved ones are worried about him or her, and that there are a number of places and people willing to help. A substance abuse prevention counselor from school will listen, and organizations like Al-Anon and Alateen can provide information about alcohol and drug problems. If the friend does not take steps to end a drinking problem, it may be necessary to tell a trusted adult about the situation.

The Yellow Pages in the phone book can also provide some names

ALATEEN

It may seem hard to believe, but alcoholism has only been recognized as a disease for about half of a century. An organization called Al-Anon has been providing help for family members of alcoholics for nearly as long. Alateen, a special group of the Al-Anon organization, helps children and teenagers who are coping with an alcoholic friend or relative. There are more than 1,500 Alateen groups in the United States, whose members are on average about 14 years old, though some may be as young as 10 and as old as 18.

Alateen does not offer counseling to its members; instead, it operates on the premise that teens and other family members affected by alcoholism will benefit from sharing their experiences in a place where everyone's privacy is protected. Al-Anon offers the same supportive environment to adults who may be coping with a child's alcoholism.

Alateen is a 12-step program, modeled on the program developed by Alcoholics Anonymous. Twelve-step programs encourage members to carry out each specific step in the outline before moving on to the next one. They also ask individuals to surrender themselves to a higher power for guidance.

Whom can Alateen help? Teenagers who know someone who drinks and answer yes to any of the following questions can receive help from this organization:

- Do you believe no one could possibly understand how you feel?

- Do you cover up your real feelings by pretending you don't care?

- Do you feel nobody really loves you or cares what happens to you?

- Do you tell lies to cover up for some one else's drinking or what's happening in your home?

- Do you stay out of the house as much as possible because you hate it there?

- Are you afraid or embarrassed to bring your friends home?

- Has someone's drinking upset you?

- Are holidays and gatherings spoiled because of drinking or others' reactions to the drinking?

- Are you afraid to speak up sometimes for fear it will set off a drinking bout or start another fight?

- Do you think the drinker's behavior is caused by you, other members of your family, friends, or rotten breaks in life?

- Do you make threats such as, "If you don't stop drinking and fighting, I'll run away"?

- Do you make promises about behavior, such as, you'll "get better grades," "go to church," or "keep the bedroom clean" in exchange for a promise that the drinking and fighting will stop?

- Do you feel that if your mom or dad loved you, she or he would stop drinking?

- Do you ever threaten or actually hurt yourself to scare your parents into saying "I'm sorry" or "I love you"?

- Do you or your family have money problems because of someone else's drinking?

- Are mealtimes frequently stressful or delayed because of drinking or fighting?

- Have you considered calling the police because of the abusive behavior in your home?

- Have you refused dates because your date may find out about the drinking or fighting?

- Do you think your problems would be solved if the drinking stopped?

- Do you ever treat people (teachers, schoolmates, teammates) unjustly because you are angry at someone else for drinking too much?

of professionals who may be helpful. There should be several entries under the headings of alcohol counselors, drug counselors, and alcohol treatment centers. It would be best to consult someone with the proper credentials, such as an NCADC (National Certified Alcohol and Drug Counselor), MAC (Master Addiction Counselor), or ICADC (International Certified Alcohol and Drug Counselor).

A Gallup Youth Survey in 1996 revealed that one out of four teenagers said that drinking was a problem in the family. Of the 507 teenagers surveyed, 44 percent said they often discussed drinking with their parents while 29 percent said they thought their parents brought the subject up too often. About 10 percent of the young people said some of those discussions escalated into arguments.

It is very unlikely that anyone with a serious drinking problem can stop on their own without the assistance of an outside counselor. To give up alcohol, heavy drinkers will have to live through alcohol withdrawal symptoms, whose management is best left to a physician. People whose bodies have grown dependent on alcohol run into potentially life-threatening trouble when they suddenly quit drinking. In the 48- to 96-hour period after they have their last drink they may shake, experience confusion, hallucinate, have a rapid heartbeat, sweat, run a fever, and have convulsions. These symptoms are collectively referred to as *delirium tremens* and can persist for as long as 10 days. While many people do not experience these symptoms, those who do are best treated in the hospital where they can be closely monitored, sedated, and given intravenous fluids.

More than 100,000 teenagers between ages 12 and 17 enter substance abuse treatment every year, according to the Substance Abuse and Mental Health Services Administration. Of those who return to their former high schools after treatment, 80 percent will begin drinking again as soon as they begin hanging out with their old friends who drink.

One way students avoid this common temptation is to enroll in special schools set up to facilitate recovery from substance

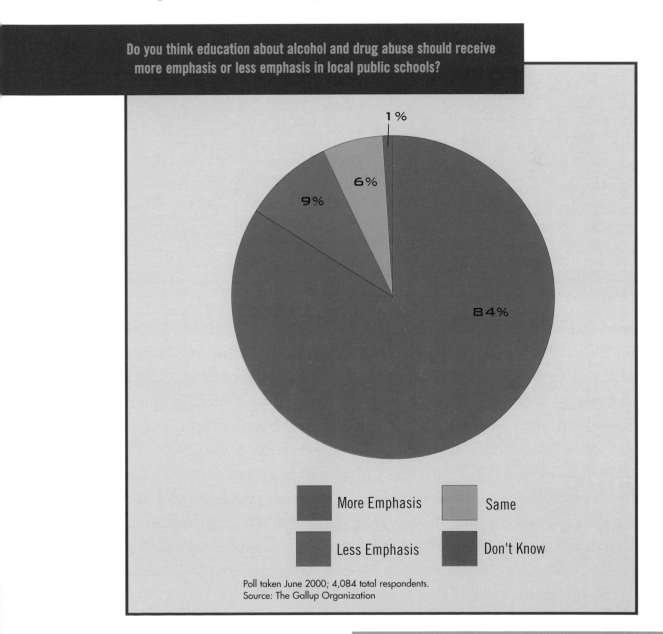

Do you think education about alcohol and drug abuse should receive more emphasis or less emphasis in local public schools?

1%

6%

9%

84%

More Emphasis

Same

Less Emphasis

Don't Know

Poll taken June 2000; 4,084 total respondents.
Source: The Gallup Organization

Friends and parents of teenage alcoholics are encouraged to confront them about their problems, but are also warned that alcoholics may act defensively or deny their problem.

abuse. There are 19 such high schools across the United States, with four more set to open by 2005. There are also three programs at the college level. These recovery schools are sometimes called dry highs, sober highs, and recovery highs. They generally have anywhere from 6 to 70 students, and everyone who is enrolled at the school is dealing in some way with substance abuse. Some of the teachers and administrators are also in recovery. Students do not live at these schools, but they receive constant support for conquering their addictions along with academic instruction. Students may be asked to take frequent urine tests and sign sobriety contracts, but they are given second chances if they relapse.

Some people believe that there should be many more recovery

schools. "Every state and most major cities could populate a recovery school, yet 40 states provide no such options," said Andy Finch, executive director of a recovery program agency that operates Community High School in Nashville, Tennessee. "I would like to see schools develop around the country so that students coming out of treatment can easily commute to a school where they can learn life skills they need to maintain their sobriety and discover that being in recovery can actually be fun."

Medicine is another tool that can help recovering alcoholics. There are currently two drugs approved by the U.S. Food and Drug Administration for treating alcoholics: disulfiram and naltrexone. Patients who take disulfiram tablets become physically ill when they drink. A drawback, though, is that patients realize that they can continue drinking by simply discontinuing the tablets. Naltrexone is used as a relapse avoidance drug. Patients begin taking it after they have stopped drinking. It works by interfering with endorphins—the body's natural feel-good chemicals that produce an alcohol high. The drug can also reduce a person's cravings for alcohol.

A new drug developed for epilepsy, topiramate, appears to also hold promise for treating alcohol withdrawal. Scientists believe the anti-seizure drug rids the brain of excess dopamine, another chemical released during intoxication that induces a feeling of well-being. The medication performed well in a London-based study of 55 alcoholics, whose results were released in 2003. Half of the subjects in the study stopped drinking or sharply curtailed their drinking. People who took the drug were six times as likely to avoid alcohol for an entire month. "This finding is a major scientific advance in the treatment of alcoholism," said Domenic Ciraulo, head of psychiatry at Boston University.

Ray Litten, chief of treatment research at the U.S. National Institute on Alcohol Abuse and Alcoholism said, "It's very promising and it certainly has potential, but this is only one study and more trials need to be done." He believes that a com-

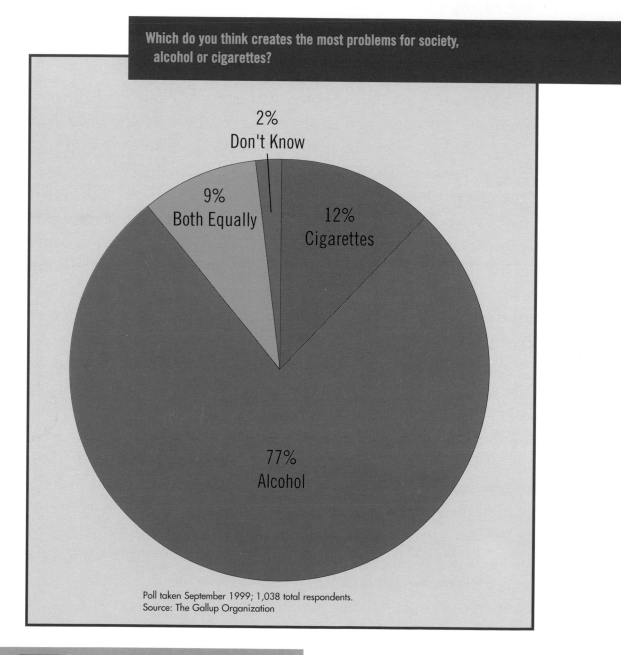

Which do you think creates the most problems for society, alcohol or cigarettes?

2%
Don't Know

9%
Both Equally

12%
Cigarettes

77%
Alcohol

Poll taken September 1999; 1,038 total respondents.
Source: The Gallup Organization

bination of medicine and psychological counseling works best to curb heavy drinking.

Dr. Bankole Johnson, chief of alcohol- and drug-addiction research at the University of Texas at San Antonio and lead investigator in the topiramate study, said any treatment that helps people cut down on the amount of alcohol they consume is beneficial. "If you can make most people stop drinking at a hazardous level, you have done them a power of good," he said. "You are going to improve these people's quality of life, help save their marriages, their jobs."

DRUG–FREE SCHOOL ZONE

HIGH PROFILE ENFORCEMENT AREA

VIOLATIONS IN THIS AREA WILL BE AGGRESSIVELY PROSECUTED

ATTORNEY GENERAL'S OFFICE DEPARTMENT OF EDUCATION

U.S. schools have a primary role in fighting underage drinking and helping students with substance abuse problems. A growing number of states have recovery schools, where teens receive personal assistance in beating their addictions.

Glossary

ADDICTION—Condition in which a person's body demands a certain substance or unpleasant symptoms will result.

ALCHEMIST—Person who practices an archaic science in which ordinary substances can be changed into something much more valuable.

DEPRESSION—Profound sadness that lasts for long periods, sometimes characterized by suicidal thoughts.

DISTILLATION—Using heat and condensation to separate gas from liquids.

FERMENTATION—Natural process that acts on yeast and sugar to produce alcohol.

FUNGI—Simple plants that don't contain chlorophyll; examples include molds, mushrooms, and mildew.

INTOXICATION—State of being drunk in which a person's mental and physical capabilities show clear impairment.

INVOLUNTARY MANSLAUGHTER—Criminal charge alleging that the defendant has unintentionally caused a death through reckless behavior.

MALT—Water-softened grain used in brewing beer and liquor.

NORM—A typical behavior serving as a standard in the community.

RECKLESS ENDANGERMENT—Criminal charge alleging an individual has exhibited behavior that placed another person at risk of bodily harm.

SCURVY—Disease caused by a lack of vitamin C whose symptoms include gum disease, loose teeth, and poor skin condition; it was frequently suffered by early sailors who had poor diets.

TEMPERANCE—Total abstinence from alcoholic beverages.

Internet Resources

http://www.gallup.com
The Gallup Organization's web page features information on the Gallup Youth Surveys as well as on the other polling work conducted by the organization.

http://www.drinksmart.org
This Canadian web site offers stories of teens who have experienced the downside of drinking. Useful sections of the site include Pubs and Parties, Alcohol Culture, and Family Forces.

http://www.recoveryschools.org
The official web site for the Association of Recovery Schools lists the locations of the schools in the 11 states where they are found. It also provides information about the recovery school experience.

http://www.al-ateen.org
This link to the Alateen and the Al-Anon organizations offers assistance to people with friends and family who are alcoholics. It also explains the purpose of the organizations as well as the 12 steps, 12 traditions, and 12 concepts.

http://www.teengetgoing.com
This Internet support group hosts online discussions about alcohol- and drug-related issues.

http://www.soberrecovery.com/links/teensinrecovery.html
This page provides links to wilderness training, camps, and other recovery organizations for teens.

Further Reading

Aaseng, Nathan. *Teens and Drunk Driving.* San Diego, Calif.: Lucent Books, 2000.

Claypool, Jane. *Alcohol and You.* New York: Franklin Watts, 1997.

Clayton, Lawrence. *Alcohol: Drug Dangers.* Berkeley Heights, N.J.: Enslow Publishers Inc., 1999.

Egendorf, Laura K., ed. *Teen Alcoholism.* San Diego, Calif.: Greenhaven Press, 2001.

Haughton, Emma. *Alcohol.* Austin, Tex.: Raintree Steck-Vaughn Publishers, 1999.

Hyde, Margaret O., and John F. Setaro. *Alcohol 101: An Overview for Teens.* Brookfield, Conn.: Twenty-First Century Books, 1999.

Kleinfeld, Judith, ed. *Fantastic Antone Grows up: Adolescents and Adults with Fetal Alcohol Syndrome.* Fairbanks: University of Alaska Press, 2000.

Kuhn, Cynthia, Scott Swartzwelder, and Wilkie Wilson. *Buzzed: The Straight Facts About the Most Used and Abused Drugs from Alcohol to Ecstasy.* New York: W.W. Norton, 1998.

Ponton, Lynn E. *The Romance of Risk: Why Teenagers Do the Things They Do.* New York: Basic Books, 1997.

Pringle, Laurence. *Drinking: A Risky Business.* New York: Morrow Junior Books, 1997.

Tate, Philip. *Alcohol: How to Give It up and Be Glad You Did.* Tucson, Ariz.: See Sharp Press, 1996.

Index

Numbers in **_bold italic_** refer to captions and graphs.

Index

Index

Index

Index/
Picture Credits

PICTURE CREDITS

Contributors

GEORGE GALLUP JR. is chairman of The George H. Gallup International Institute (sponsored by The Gallup International Research and Education Center, or GIREC) and is senior scientist and member of the GIREC council. Mr. Gallup serves as chairman of the board of the National Coalition for Children's Justice and as a trustee of the National Fatherhood Initiative. He serves on many other boards in the area of health, education and religion.

Mr. Gallup is recognized internationally for his research and study on youth, health, religion, and urban problems. He has written numerous books including *My Kids On Drugs?* with Art Linkletter (Standard, 1981), *The Great American Success Story* with Alec Gallup and William Proctor (Dow Jones-Irwin, 1986), *Growing Up Scared in America* with Wendy Plump (Morehouse, 1995), *Surveying the Religious Landscape: Trends in U.S. Beliefs* with D. Michael Lindsay (Morehouse, 1999), and *The Next American Spirituality* with Timothy Jones (Chariot Victor Publishing, 1999).

Mr. Gallup received his BA degree from the Princeton University Department of Religion in 1954, and holds seven honorary degrees. He has received many awards, including the Charles E. Wilson Award in 1994, the Judge Issacs Lifetime Achievement Award in 1996, and the Bethune-DuBois Institute Award in 2000. Mr. Gallup lives near Princeton, New Jersey, with his wife, Kingsley. They have three grown children.

THE GALLUP YOUTH SURVEY was founded in 1977 by Dr. George Gallup to provide ongoing information on the opinions, beliefs and activities of America's high school students and to help society meet its responsibility to youth. The topics examined by the Gallup Youth Survey have covered a wide range—from abortion to zoology. From its founding through the year 2001, the Gallup Youth Survey sent more than 1,200 weekly reports to the Associated Press, to be distributed to newspapers around the nation. Since January 2002, Gallup Youth Survey reports have been made available on a weekly basis through the Gallup Tuesday Briefing.

GAIL SNYDER has written several books for young readers. Her other title in the Gallup Youth Survey series is *Teens, Religion, and Values.* She has also written about George Washington's childhood and the nation of Sudan. Gail lives with her husband, Hal Marcovitz, their children Ashley and Michelle, and her father, Aaron Snyder, in Chalfont, Pennsylvania.